Doll Collecting with Tina

CLASSIC DOLLS FROM 1860 TO 1960

Tina Berry

with Francine Hornberger

Photography by George Ross

FRIEDMAN/FAIRFAX

ACKNOWLEDGMENTS

We would like to thank the proprietors of Matrix Quality Antique Dolls by Mail, Inc.,
for providing the beautiful dolls featured in this book, as well as for their editorial contributions
to the descriptions that accompany the doll portraits.

A FRIEDMAN/FAIRFAX BOOK
© 2002 by Michael Friedman Publishing Group, Inc.

Library of Congress Cataloging-in-Publication Data available upon request.

ISBN 1-58663-235-3

Editor: Susan Lauzau
Editorial Consultants: Matrix by Mail, Inc.
Art Director: Kevin Ullrich
Designer: Lindgren/Fuller Book Design
Photography Director: Chris Bain
Photography Editor: Janice Ackerman
Photography Stylist: Kathleen Wolfe
Production Manager: Richela Fabian Morgan

All photos © George Ross

Color separations by Chroma Graphics (Overseas) Pte Ltd
Printed in Italy by Milanostampa-New International

1 3 5 7 9 10 8 6 4 2

Distributed by Sterling Publishing Company, Inc.
387 Park Avenue South
New York, NY 10016
Distributed in Canada by Sterling Publishing
Canadian Manda Group
One Atlantic Avenue, Suite 105
Toronto, Ontario, Canada M6K 3E7
Distributed in Australia by
Capricorn Link (Australia) Pty, Ltd.
P.O. Box 704, Windsor, NSW 2756 Australia

CONTENTS

Introduction 4

INTRODUCTION

Aclassic doll is one whose charm has endured from the time it was first introduced to the present day. Made from a variety of materials and in hundreds of different styles, classic dolls provide a portal to a world gone by, offering a nostalgic glimpse into the past, where creativity fused with fashion to generate playthings that, in many cases, are as interesting historically as they are beautiful.

The dolls featured in this book were produced chiefly in Europe or North America between 1860 and 1960. Why these dates? For one, there aren't many pre-1860s dolls in great condition—and in an affordable price range for the majority of collectors (most of the dolls profiled in this book fall into the $100 to $5,000 range, though some more luxurious examples have been included). Also, the invention of the sewing machine in the mid-1800s expanded the doll market greatly because it made production of doll fashions and some types of dolls more efficient and inexpensive than ever before. The survey ends at 1960 because from that point, dolls intended as playthings were made almost exclusively from vinyl, and most collectors mark the modern age of doll collecting from the introduction of vinyl dolls.

A BRIEF HISTORY OF CLASSIC DOLLS

Dolls have been beloved objects for thousands of years. Archaeological digs have turned up examples from ancient Greece and Rome—dating back as far as the sixth century B.C.E. Terra-cotta pottery dolls and simple carved-wood or ivory statuettes, some with clothing carved onto the doll itself, are typical finds. While leather and cloth were also used to make dolls, most examples fashioned from these materials have disintegrated. Also exceedingly fragile were those dolls made of bone, a material popular with the ancient Egyptians. What is not documented, however, is whether these figurines were meant as toys or had some other, perhaps religious, purpose. It wasn't until the seventeenth century that dolls as we know them—playthings created exclusively for children to dress up and love—really began to be made.

The earliest of these dolls were crafted from wood and had their facial features painted on. Papier-mâché dolls, made from the beginning of the nineteenth and into the early twentieth century, became a popular alternative to wooden dolls because they were less expensive and more efficiently made. While wax dolls had existed in Europe since the Middle Ages, it wasn't until the mid-nineteenth century that these were created as toys. Before about the 1850s, the wax dolls produced were intended for adults, chiefly as decorative objects. Their popularity steadily declined until the end of the nineteenth century as more durable materials came into vogue.

Porcelain was the favorite material for doll heads from the middle to the end of the nineteenth century. It was either used glazed, for china dolls, or unglazed, for bisque dolls. (Parian dolls are a type of bisque doll. They are set apart, however, because traditional bisque heads are tinted, while parian heads are not.) The beauty of porcelain, not to mention its hardness and durability, made it the natural material of choice for doll heads from the mid to late 1800s. Another benefit was that it could be easily cleaned, unlike its papier-mâché and wax predecessors.

Entire bodies made from any of the above materials, although they existed, were unrealistic as playthings for children. Dolls' bodies needed to be soft and malleable. So while heads were made from wood, papier-mâché, wax, or porcelain, bodies were made from cloth, leather, or gutta-percha, a tough plastic substance that resembles rubber. Sawdust-filled fabric was common for mass-produced dolls.

Fashion dolls dominated the doll scene in the second half of the nineteenth century. But by the 1880s, they were pushed aside for the next new craze: the bébé, a doll made in the image of a small child. While some childlike dolls existed before the late nineteenth century, most produced up to that point were miniature depictions of adults. Bébés were extremely appealing because they gave young girls a new element of play. While exquisite fashionable clothing continued to be produced, allowing girls the pleasure of dressing their bébés up in glamorous clothing, the girls could pretend to be mommies to these dolls. Bébés dominated the doll industry until the middle of the 1950s, when fashion dolls came back into vogue with the introduction of Ginny, Little Miss Revlon, and others. The most famous fashion doll, of course, is Barbie, who took the world by storm at the beginning of the 1960s (because Barbie belongs to the modern doll era, this book does not profile her individually).

As the desire to mass produce dolls became greater, porcelain was set aside for newer, less expensive materials. In the beginning of the twentieth century, composition took over as the material of choice, especially in the United States. In fact, the introduction of composition at last made the U.S. a major player in the doll market, which had previously been dominated by France and Germany. Celluloid was also a popular material, but as its flaws (chiefly flammability) were shown to outweigh its qualities, it soon fell out of favor.

By the 1930s, the newest craze was for character dolls, composition dolls molded to look like characters invented by the doll manufacturer or like top celebrities of the day, including Shirley Temple, Fanny Brice, Deanna Durbin, and others. Although character dolls are no longer made from composition, dolls molded in the image of celebrities are top sellers even today.

In the 1940s, during World War II, hard plastic began to replace composition as the material of choice because of its nearly indestructible nature. But by the end of the 1950s, hard plastic, too, was being replaced by the more huggable vinyl, which has remained the material of choice for doll making.

A CLOSER LOOK AT MATERIALS

A dollmaker's reasons for selecting one material over another vary, with considerations ranging from the inherent beauty and true-to-life qualities of the material to its durability, availability, and/or affordability. In the following sections we'll discuss the materials from which the majority of classic dolls were made, but be aware that other materials do exist—including rubber, aluminum, and fabric.

Wood

Wooden dolls may be carved or constructed entirely from wood, but more often "wooden" denotes a doll with a beautifully carved wooden head, a painted face, and a body of leather, cloth, or even rubber. Because wood is essentially durable, many early examples exist—some even dating from ancient times. Wood was a very common material for doll making because even the poorest doll lover could carve an image into an inexpensive or found piece of wood. By the end of the eighteenth century, wood lost some of its popularity to wax—even though wood, for the most part, held up better than wax—because wax was more lifelike, both in tone and in texture.

Papier-Mâché

Another popular doll-making material of the nineteenth century, papier-mâché was in common use because it was accessible, easy to make, and inexpensive, too. While this material—made from paper pulp, water, glue, and other additives—was being used to create doll heads as early as the sixteenth century, the first patent for a papier-mâché doll head was not issued until 1858.

The major attraction of papier-mâché for dollmakers was that, by the nineteenth century, it could be pressure-molded to create mass-produced doll heads. This technology had an enormous impact on elevating Germany to the status of a doll-making empire. And because papier-mâché dolls were much cheaper to produce than porcelain ones, production of papier-mâché dolls remained steady well into the twentieth century. The major drawback: if not properly treated, papier-mâché is quite fragile. For this reason, very few of the earliest examples exist today, and the ones that survived from the nineteenth and early twentieth centuries are rarely found in top condition.

Wax

Wax has been used for centuries to create lifelike dolls, but, like papier-mâché, the fragility of the material means that there are not many early examples to be found today.

There are three main types of wax dolls. Poured-wax dolls, made by filling a mold with wax (a method that originated in Great Britain), were very popular in the late eighteenth and early nineteenth centuries. Wax-over dolls, made by dipping papier-mâché forms into wax, started to gain popularity around 1840. Reinforced-wax dolls—which feature a wax head reinforced from the inside with a thin layer of plaster of Paris—were made in Germany between 1860 and 1890.

Wax dolls of all types began to wane in popularity when sturdier materials, such as porcelain, were introduced.

Porcelain

True porcelain is made from a mix of kaolin, a fine white clay, and petuntse, a type of feldspar, fired at a very high temperature. This is also known as hard-paste porcelain, and the method was first developed in China. Soft-paste porcelain was created by Europeans as they searched for the secret of making hard-paste porcelain; made from fine clay and glasslike substances, it has a creamier color than true porcelain and is less durable. Bone china, which incorporates bone ash into the kaolin/petuntse mix, is not as hard as true porcelain, but is more durable than soft-paste porcelain.

Valued for its whiteness, thinness, and translucence, porcelain is today considered quite delicate, but when porcelain doll heads were introduced in the mid 1800s, they were welcomed for their relative durability. Wax and papier-mâché dolls were nearly impossible to clean without damaging the doll, but porcelain was easy to wash. Consumers didn't mind paying extra for a doll that wouldn't be ruined by soiling.

In addition to the various types of porcelain, there are a number of different finishes commonly used for dolls, including glazed porcelain, commonly called china; unglazed porcelain, known as bisque; and an unglazed, untinted porcelain called parian. Bisque was a preferred material, because its matte surface created a more lifelike appearance, especially when tinted.

Celluloid

Celluloid became an especially popular material for dolls during the early part of the twentieth century due to its supposedly indestructible nature. Made of soluble cellulose, nitrate, and camphor, celluloid looked great when it was new but didn't age gracefully. Also, it proved extremely flammable when exposed to heat or when sealed away in a box, and by the 1940s, it became illegal to use celluloid for doll production in the United States.

Although it remained extremely popular with German and Japanese doll manufacturers for some time, celluloid started to fall out of favor in the doll-making industry when composition began to dominate.

Composition

Composition, a material made from a mixture of sawdust, glue, and wood pulp, actually appeared right before the turn of the twentieth century, but didn't gain popularity for more than a decade. The main draw of composition dolls was that they were inexpensive to make, and entire doll bodies could be fabricated from the same material as the heads. These dolls were also thought to be unbreakable. A look at the composition dolls that have survived to the present day may support that supposition, but it also shows that they are not invincible. Composition dolls are susceptible to damage as they age, and from excessive heat or cold. Typical signs of this damage include crazing (a network of fine cracks across the surface), lines around the eyes and mouth, and crackling of the eyes.

Hard Plastic

Perfected during World War II, hard plastic replaced composition as the ideal material for making dolls when the war ended. Not only was it an ideal weight for doll making, it could also be easily molded, painted, and washed. Unlike composition, it was not susceptible to crazing and could withstand extremes of temperature and exposure to moisture.

Vinyl

The most common material used for doll making from the middle of the 1950s through the present day is vinyl. It can be hard or soft, is less expensive to produce than plastic, can be easily dyed, and has a more natural feel than hard plastic.

COLLECTING BASICS

One very popular place to find and enjoy classic dolls is a doll show. Here, you'll be able to see a wide array of dolls all at once and get a sense of what you'd like to collect, while at the same time gaining an understanding of how the same type of doll can fluctuate enormously in value, depending on its condition. You'll also be able to meet many doll dealers and forge relationships, making alliances with dealers you can trust.

Another alternative is to scour the papers for local garage sales and estate sales. If you are patient, you may come across a gem at one of these venues. Doll auctions are another option. If you have internet access, check out the various online auction sites, such as eBay, for dolls. Be cautious when buying online, however, because unlike an "in-the-box" contemporary doll, a classic doll can possess value-diminishing flaws that are easily missed without careful inspection. Your best bet is always to handle a doll before purchasing.

Lastly, you may decide to join an antique doll collector's club or association. These groups are beneficial in that they can help you identify what you want to collect—and present a whole group of new eyes to help you seek out the treasures you're after.

Whether you are a novice doll collector or have been collecting for years, use the following guide to help build and maintain your collection.

Identification

Antique dolls are generally collected by manufacturer and year, and this information is usually ascertained by markings on the doll. Typically located on the back of the head as well as the torso, each identifying mark is linked with a particular manufacturer. This is not always a reliable way to identify a classic doll, however. Before the middle of the nineteenth century, many dolls were produced without marks.

The more acquainted you become with antique dolls, the more you will be able to identify a look, an eye treatment, or a facial expression with a particular type of doll or doll manufacturer. Proceed with caution, however. Many reproductions of antique dolls exist, and it may be difficult to determine whether a doll is authentic without the identifying marks. Thoroughly research the dolls you want to buy and be certain that the antique or vintage doll you want to purchase has the proper features and marks for a doll of its age and manufacture.

Condition

The value of a classic doll is greatly affected by its condition. Unlike modern collectible dolls, the dolls of the distant past weren't kept in a box, stored safely away, with the hope that they'd one day increase in value. Doll owners in earlier times were mainly children, who invariably played with their dolls. And the more loved the doll, the more worn out it became. While it is nearly impossible to find an antique doll in perfect condition, there are criteria of condition that set one doll apart from another in terms of monetary value.

Following are a few guidelines. A crack or repair to the head of a bisque doll will diminish its value by roughly 50 to 60 percent, whereas a body in poor condition will affect the value of the doll by only about 20 percent. For wax dolls, value can be diminished by 20 to 80 percent, depending on how severe cracks or warps to the head are. If the doll is rewaxed, however, figure about 70 percent diminished value. Because it's a fact of life that papier-mâché and composition dolls will crack, split, and peel, even the worst-case scenario of any of these means approximately only 30 percent diminished value. But heavy chipping to the face not associated with normal wear and tear will diminish the value by as much as 75 percent, while a repainted face can knock as much as 80 percent off the value of the doll. If a plastic doll is cracked or discolored, expect a reduction of 40 percent in the value. A celluloid doll that is cracked or discolored will lose 70 to 80 percent of its value.

Remember that each doll is unique, and that while certain flaws will greatly affect the value of a doll, some may have little or no effect at all. Be sure to acquaint yourself with all the factors that influence the value of the doll you are looking to acquire, and take the time to thoroughly examine any antique doll before you buy.

Repair

As the value factors mentioned previously indicate, sometimes it is best to leave a doll alone. As with any type of antique, a repair, such as rewaxing or repainting, can actually diminish a doll's value. When purchasing a doll or having one repaired, keep this in mind—or you may end up with a pretty, clean doll that has little or no value at all. While many repairs will not affect the value of a doll dramatically—for example, a small paint touchup on the face of a wooden doll or the careful washing of a doll's clothes—most are best done only if absolutely necessary and should be left to professional doll doctors.

Care

Proper storage of your dolls depends on the type of doll you collect. All dolls must be kept out of direct sunlight and away from excessive heat, cold, humidity, and dryness. Take care to wrap wooden dolls in tissue paper for storage so they don't rub up against each other and cause chipping and splintering. If they are on display, try not to move them around too much for the same reason.

Papier-mâché should be stored carefully in a safe place—the severe temperature fluctuations likely in a basement or attic mean that these spots are not safe havens for your papier-mâché dolls. It is not recommended that you clean them.

Wax dolls should, first and foremost, be kept away from any heat source, be it a sunny window, a heating duct or radiator, or a fireplace. They should be cleaned using only the gentlest materials. Many experts recommend nothing harsher than a cotton swab dipped in a gentle detergent (such as Woolite) and cool water.

Porcelain is easily cleaned (a major reason for its appeal when first introduced). For the sake of the doll's face, be sure to clean only with a nonabrasive cleanser that is free of any bleach.

Avoid cleaning celluloid dolls altogether, if possible. And, because of their highly combustible nature, never store them in a sealed container.

Be careful when cleaning composition dolls. While fine lines and crazing are acceptable for the most part, you don't want to do more harm than good when cleaning your doll. Try cleaning with petroleum jelly and a soft tissue, being careful to avoid painted eyelashes and brows, which are easily wiped away. If you don't think you're getting enough dirt off, just leave it alone. A slightly soiled doll will command more than a bleached or peeling one.

Hard plastic and vinyl are easily cleaned with soap and water, but avoid cleansers that contain chlorine bleach or ammonia. Be especially careful to avoid excessive heat and direct sunlight with these dolls, and keep vinyl dolls away from fluorescent lighting, which can eventually discolor and damage the dolls.

✂

The reasons people collect antique dolls are varied and diverse, but whether you collect to relive warm childhood memories, to make a solid financial investment, or simply to enjoy the beauty that these miniature beauties impart, enter into the hobby properly prepared. Learning everything you can about the dolls you want to collect will help you to acquire a collection that you will cherish and enjoy, and perhaps be able to profit from.

This book offers background for nearly a hundred years of classic dolls, discussing trends in doll making throughout the decades, world events that affected these trends, and the influential manufacturers in the doll industry. You'll also find a gallery of classic and collectible dolls that illustrate many of these trends and represent the finest dollmakers. We hope that this information will help you decide which dolls you want to collect and guide you through this exciting pastime.

A NOTE ABOUT THE ESTIMATED VALUES

The estimated values attached to the dolls in this book reflect the broad price range or approximate value for which a collector might expect to find a doll of that type and condition (the dolls featured in this book are nearly all in excellent or mint condition; any elements that might detract from its value have been noted). Remember that condition is an important factor in determining a particular doll's value, and that relative rarity of specific sizes, wig colors, costumes, and the like can greatly affect the market value of a doll. In addition, a doll wearing original clothing, possessing marks and/or original tags, or one complete with box and accompanying accessories will command a higher price. Because of the great number of variables taken into account when assessing a doll's value, it is always best to have your doll appraised by a professional.

CHAPTER I

1860 – 1869

The 1860s was a decade of turmoil, a period in which vast changes swept North America. In 1860, the Pony Express mail system began, which eventually gave way to the ever-expanding telegraph network—both these innovations widened the world by allowing people to communicate more quickly and efficiently than ever before. Perhaps most significantly from 1861 to 1866, the Civil War divided the nation, causing lasting rifts among families, shifting political and social realities, and, for some, changing an entire way of life. The decade also saw the assassination of one president and the near impeachment of another.

But overseas, life was moving at a slower pace. It was a quiet time in Europe, historically speaking, so more energy and effort could be devoted to the small pleasures of life. It was in the 1860s that French manufacturers took the doll world by storm with gorgeous fashion dolls, which they called *Poupee de Mode.*

Paris has long been the center of the fashion universe, so it is only natural that fashion dolls were initially produced there. Most of the owners of these dolls were children from well-to-do families, which is not surprising when you consider how expensive these dolls could be due to all the work that went into making them. Fashion dolls were always extravagantly dressed, down to their lace-trimmed undergarments.

Rohmer fashion doll, circa 1865

Clothing was often made from luxury materials, including silk, cashmere, and velvet, but was sometimes sewn from more basic fabrics such as cotton, wool, and muslin. So large was the demand for these beautifully dressed fashion dolls, in fact, that an entire industry sprang up to create their clothing and accessories in the Passage Choiseul section of Paris.

While fashion dolls had been produced much earlier, this new class of dolls featured one important difference: the heads were made from porcelain, a material that wasn't new, but had only recently begun to be used for dolls' heads. Porcelain was easy to clean and more durable than wax or papier-mâché, and the doll heads created from this material appeared more delicate, and therefore, more beautiful. These dolls' heads were made either from glazed china or from unglazed tinted china. The latter, commonly known as bisque, became the most popular material for creating doll heads well into the twentieth century because of its true-to-life quality.

Interestingly, while doll bodies and elaborate costumes were made in France, the heads were typically manufactured in Germany. Germany didn't join France whole-heartedly in the fashion doll–making effort until the 1870s. Once German dollmakers ventured into the manufacture of complete dolls, makers in France and Germany set the standard of excellence for the rest of the world.

While there were many manufacturers of these delightful fashion dolls, those most collected and treasured today can be attributed to just a few dollmakers. The top producer was Jumeau, a dollmaker that had produced fashion dolls as early as 1842, but with heads of wax, wood, or papier-mâche. In the 1860s, Jumeau began producing porcelain-headed dolls, and the dolls they produced in this period are beyond compare.

Several companies run by women, unusual for the 1860s, operated on a smaller scale than Jumeau but nonetheless produced some of the most beautiful fashion dolls of the era. Adelaide Calixte Huret first won acclaim with a beautiful jointed doll, which won a silver medal at an international exhibition in 1855. By 1860, she had established her own Paris-based porcelain factory. Her firm, Maison Huret, produced only about 1500 dolls per year, but her dolls were always well received, winning awards for fashion as well as for innovations in body design and construction. Leontine Rohmer became Mlle. Huret's main competition in the 1860s, when she began producing fashion dolls exclusively. Unhappy with the resemblance Rohmer's dolls bore to her own, Mlle. Huret took legal action against Rohmer, and the production of Rohmer dolls ceased by 1880. Despite the small window of time in which

THE JUMEAU DOLL COMPANY

One of the top producers of fashion dolls, Jumeau was founded in Paris as Belton and Jumeau, a small doll-making shop, in 1842. The two partners, M. Belton and Pierre Francois Jumeau, created exquisite fashion dolls with leather bodies and heads made from wood, papier-mâché, or wax. Within a couple of years, the pair was creating award-winning dolls that were exported throughout the world. When Belton died in 1846, Jumeau was left on his own. Pierre Jumeau, followed by his son, Emile, continued to make prized dolls, however, for decades to come.

Unlike many manufacturers of the time, Jumeau understood that there was a ready market for dolls that were affordable for people other than the wealthy. In response to this need, he created simpler dolls that were dressed impeccably, if not quite as elegantly. This move to manufacture for the masses meant higher production rates and sales of his fashion dolls, ensuring a strong hold on the doll market.

In 1860, Jumeau followed the trend to create fashion dolls with porcelain heads. While at first he, like many French doll producers of the day, imported the doll heads from factories in Germany, Jumeau eventually saw the wisdom of creating his own heads, and opened his own porcelain factory in 1873.

Through the years, Jumeau produced exquisite dolls that were most revered for their clothing. He was also known to sell dolls without clothing, in which case he marketed the clothing separately.

Pierre Jumeau retired at the end of the 1870s, just as the fashion doll craze gave way to the new bébés. Pierre's son, Emile, armed with his father's business savvy and strong sense of what the doll-buying public sought, resolved to make the company the top doll manufacturer in the world and began producing the masterful bébés so eagerly sought by collectors today.

Rohmer dolls were produced—only about twenty years—those that have survived are in very high demand by collectors.

Bru, formally Jne Bru & Cie, produced delightful fashion dolls around the end of the 1860s. Because of the small numbers produced, these dolls are especially coveted by collectors today. The company, led by Leon Casimir Bru, would become more famous for its bébés in the following decades.

Another growing trend, which later became a full-blown craze, originated in the 1860s: the celluloid doll, which was first introduced at the decade's end. Celluloid dolls were extremely desirable because of their supposedly indestructible nature, a claim that would ultimately prove false. The manufacture of celluloid dolls became prodigious in Germany in the next decade, and was yet another factor that made Germany a world-renowned producer of classic dolls.

In the mid-1800s, a novel invention was unveiled. Christened "automata," these were dolls that were able to move on their own. A Parisian watchmaker, Jules Nicholas Steiner, ignited the passion for animated dolls in 1855, when he obtained a patent for a mechanical doll that could walk and speak. The doll was wound by a key on its hip and, according to the language of the patent, it could move its head, hips, arms, legs, and lips, and could even scream when lying down. By 1867, Steiner patented another doll—this one, instead of screaming, made squeaking noises generated by a voice box implanted in its cloth torso. By 1869, he had also invented a doll that could roll about on wheels.

In the decades that followed, automata became a staple for many dollmakers, including Bru and Jumeau. The phenomenon would remain one of the biggest crazes in doll making until the dawn of the twentieth century, then would disappear almost entirely after the First World War. But until the demise of automata, the dolls produced amazed and astounded the public with the remarkable things they could do.

Wax doll, circa 1860

PIEROTTI, ENGLAND

ESTIMATED VALUE: $3,000

The Pierotti family made and distributed wax dolls from the 1780s until well into the 1930s. Founded by Domenico Pierotti, the company continued over time to use many of its original molds to create its dolls, giving even the later dolls a sense of the antique. Pierotti dolls were typically made of poured wax, with soft features and hair of rooted mohair. Many bore a signature Pierotti trait: their heads were typically cocked slightly to one side.

Poured-wax dolls generally took a great deal of time to produce, which limited quantities, and for this reason, poured-wax dolls can be worth considerably more than reinforced-wax and wax-over dolls. A twenty-four-inch (61cm) wax doll of exceptional quality can be valued as high as $3,500, but one of only average quality may command a price in the range of $1,400.

This twenty-four-inch poured-wax example has rooted mohair hair and inset glass eyes. Her body is cloth with three-quarters poured-wax arms and legs. The body is signed by the manufacturer, which adds to the value of the doll. Her shoes are genuine leather and her clothes are all original. This doll is in excellent condition.

Wax doll, circa 1860

CREMER, ENGLAND

ESTIMATED VALUE: $3,000—$3,500

Cremer is a little known but well regarded dollmaker based in England. This is an extremely rare Cremer wax doll, which accounts for the value placed on it. In fact, any wax doll in such good condition is an exceptional treasure. Wax has a tendency to crack or warp, unfortunate problems that can diminish the value of the doll by as much as 80 percent, depending on the extent of the damage to the wax and the clothing. This doll has a poured-wax head with a cloth body and three-quarter, poured-wax limbs. Not many wax dolls are signed by the maker, as is this Cremer. Her hair is rooted mohair and her eyes are blue glass. She is wearing her original clothing.

China doll, circa 1860

MAKER UNVERIFIED, GERMANY

ESTIMATED VALUE: $1,500

German makers were undisputedly leaders in doll manufacturing and distribution in the latter half of the nineteenth century, and their china dolls are well loved for their painted blue eyes, full cheeks (often painted a rose color), and small closed mouths. German china dolls of this period were made with a china head and a body of cloth or leather. The arms and legs on these shoulder-head dolls were either glazed china, cloth, or leather. The beautiful example shown here has a head and lower arms and legs of glazed porcelain; her body is stuffed cloth. Her hair is a desirable color and she boasts a molded snood. She wears a brocaded two-part ensemble evocative of her day.

Early fashion doll, circa 1865

MME. ROHMER, FRANCE

ESTIMATED VALUE: $7,500–$10,000

Rohmer dolls are noted for their high quality, as well as for their incredible beauty. A trailblazer in doll manufacturing, Mme. Leontine Rohmer not only forged new paths as a successful businesswoman at a time when that term was almost unheard of, she also registered several patents, most significantly a doll head that pivoted on a metal rod. Her husband was a mechanic who aided her in making improvements to her dolls, which other manufacturers in the industry ultimately borrowed. The Rohmer mark is recognizable by its oval shape, which bears Mme. Rohmer's name on the top arc and "Breveté SGDG Paris" across the bottom.

The exceptional doll featured here is one of Mme. Rohmer's glazed porcelain fashion dolls, and is in excellent condition, particularly for a doll of her age. Her head and shoulders are of glazed porcelain, as are her three-quarter arms, while the tops of her arms (to her shoulders) and the remainder of her body are made from kid leather. She has early cobalt blue glass eyes and wears a light brown wig made from human hair. Her eyelashes and eyebrows are hand-painted with individual strokes. All original, her lavender and cream costume is made from stiff net.

Automaton, circa 1865

ALEXANDER NICHOLAS THEROUDE, FRANCE

ESTIMATED VALUE: $3,000–$5,000

The Theroude doll company produced mainly key-wound walking and talking dolls between 1837 and 1895. Alexander Theroude registered his first patent in 1848 for a doll that stood on a wheeled platform and featured a turning head and eyes that opened and closed. The circa-1865 automaton shown here is sixteen inches (40.5cm) tall, an unusual size—most automata are smaller toys, typically ranging from nine to twelve inches (23–30.5cm). This doll is in remarkably good condition given the fact that this type of automaton is prone to tipping, which can cause damage to the face—with a papier-mâché doll, like this example, damage can be especially significant. A simple key-wind mechanical, this doll moves to the left or right, depending on the direction in which the front wheel is turned; note that a mechanism on wheels is responsible for the doll's movements rather than the figure itself. The doll's head and body are made from papier-mâché, except for her arms, which are leather. Her body is stiff-jointed, and she has two upper and two lower teeth, and stationary black glass eyes. Her linen clothing is not original, but it is appropriate for a baby or toddler doll of the era.

CHAPTER 2

1870 — 1879

The 1870s saw Europe at war and the United States finally at peace. In the early part of the decade, the Franco-Prussian War was being fought—this conflict had far-reaching effects, some of which would ultimately set off World War 1. The 1870s in the United States was a quieter time, but there were a number of notable occurrences: the first pneumatic-powered subway line opened to the public in New York City, Levi Strauss patented his soon-to-be-world-famous blue jeans, and Jesse James committed the world's first train robbery. It was also an important decade for technological innovation. Alexander Graham Bell invented the telephone and Thomas Edison invented and patented the electric light bulb and the phonograph. It was the latter invention, the phonograph, that proved to be an enormous asset to makers of the mechanical dolls known as automata.

Once Jules Steiner, developer of the first mechanicals, received his patent and began to develop his animated dolls, it was only a matter of time until others followed suit. While the French Steiner continued to develop more dolls and apply for additional patents, dollmakers in other parts of the world advanced the technology in their own ways. In the United States in the 1860s, Enoch Rice Morrison patented the first real walking doll, a doll that was able to take tiny steps with the

Fashion doll, 1875

help of a small clockwork mechanism. A very similar doll was also patented in England around the same time. These dolls were known as *autoperipatikos*, Greek for "to go by oneself," and typically featured heads made of wax or bisque.

These new dolls paved the way for the next wave of mechanical dolls that could crawl, dance, and even swim. Over the course of the next few decades, each new mechanical outperformed the previous one, and all the major doll manufacturers jumped on the trend. Bru acquired a patent in 1872 for a doll that had two faces and a music box. The company later developed dolls that could "eat," "drink," "breathe," and even "sleep."

In the late 1860s and through 1870s, French doll manufacturers Roullet & Decamps were perhaps the best-known maker of walking dolls. The most famous invention of this team, however, would not come until years later, when they invented *Le Fumeur*, The Smoker, a doll that actually smoked through a hole located in its right arm. When the cigarette was raised to the doll's mouth, the figure appeared to be smoking, but the smoke actually traveled through the arm and into a bellows in the body. The bellows then pushed the smoke out through the mouth, creating the effect of exhaling. Roullet & Decamps only produced the mechanisms themselves, purchasing other parts to create their dolls from manufacturers such as Jumeau. So while there are automata that bear the Jumeau stamp, the company did not produce such mechanical dolls at this point; rather, Roullet & Decamps built their dolls with Jumeau pieces.

The invention of the phonograph revolutionized the market for automata by allowing dolls to make a more complex set of sounds. Originally, dolls "talked" via voice box mechanisms implanted in the torso; after the invention of the phonograph, voices could be recorded and played back. Instead of the standard "mama," it was now possible for a doll to have a complete vocabulary. Although Edison patented his talking doll in 1878, it wasn't until the 1890s that he brought it to market. The doll proved too expensive for most consumers, however, and soon disappeared until Jumeau introduced its talking doll a few years later.

Despite the technological innovations of the 1870s, the treasured bisque and china fashion dolls had not lost their popularity. In fact, it was during this decade that German makers embraced this market wholeheartedly and began producing complete dolls instead of only the heads they had been famous for in previous decades. In addition to an amazing catalog of porcelain dolls, Germany also began to lead in the production of celluloid dolls.

JOEL ELLIS AND HIS WOODEN DOLLS

❧

While the heyday of wooden dolls was long past by the 1870s, one producer of these seeming throwbacks made a big splash in the one-year period in which he produced his dolls. In that short time, he managed to put the United States, at last, on the map of respected doll-making countries. Joel Ellis's wooden dolls are recognized today as the first commercially produced American dolls.

Joel Addison Hartley Ellis ran the Co-Operative Manufacturing Company in Vermont between 1873 and 1874. In that time, he patented several new features that were widely used for dolls that were not necessarily made from wood. Unique to any doll of the day, Joel Ellis's wooden dolls were made using a mortise-and-tenon construction, which gave them a range of motion never before enjoyed by a doll. The bodies were made from rock maple, and the hands and feet from cast iron, pewter, or other metals. The limbs were turned on a lathe and the heads, made by steaming and compressing blocks of wood, were attached to the bodies on a dowel.

It is unclear why Ellis gave up his doll-making efforts after only one year, as he lived until 1925. Whatever Ellis's reasons for ceasing production, the fact that so few of his dolls exist makes them highly desirable. The main drawback of the Joel Ellis dolls is that they have not stood the test of time. Many are marred by peeling or flaking paint, or have been repainted, thus significantly decreasing their value.

Johann Daniel Kestner, the self-proclaimed "king of dollmakers," was the largest producer of German bisque dolls in the 1870s and 1880s. Kestner began his empire making papier-mâché dolls by 1820. In 1822, the German government had granted him a ten-year monopoly on the production of papier-mâché dolls in exchange for his assistance in helping the poor by providing food and employment in the poverty-stricken region where his business was located. This monopoly helped firmly establish Kestner as a successful dollmaker, and he continued as a maker of note through most of the nineteenth century.

Established in 1870, the Simon & Halbig Porcelain Factory mainly produced and exported porcelain doll heads, but as the decade progressed the company began to move steadily toward creating complete dolls. In addition to producing its own dolls, Simon & Halbig introduced several innovations, including eyes that moved via a lever, eyes that opened and closed, and eyelashes made from thread. Early Simon & Halbig dolls featured molded hair, but as the trend after 1870 was to use wigs, the company soon followed suit.

Dollmakers in other countries—the United States and Great Britain among them—saw the immense potential in the market and began to copy the European manufacturers, but the dolls produced in these other nations could not match the magnificence of the French and German dolls. Some of these European dolls were so exquisite that they could command extraordinarily high prices. In 1872, for example, a Bru doll was advertised as costing from $6.00 to $100.00, depending upon the outfit the doll was wearing.

By the end of the 1870s, the appeal of fashion dolls had begun to wane. A new type of doll caught the public's fancy and increased dramatically in popularity in the late 1870s. Bébés, dolls designed to look like small children, began to win over little girls around the world, who set aside their grown-up fashion ladies to play mommy to these charming childlike dolls.

Wax doll, 1870

MONTANARI, ENGLAND

ESTIMATED VALUE: $2,000–$2,500

Augusta Montanari produced her exceptional wax dolls in England between 1851 and 1884. She is purportedly responsible for creating the Royal Model Dolls, modeled on the children of Queen Victoria, though many other dollmakers have also laid claim to these dolls.

The wax child doll pictured here is dressed as an infant in an elaborate christening ensemble, and features a cloth body with wax arms (from the elbows) and wax legs (from the knees). She is in extraordinarily good condition, which gives her added value. Her lavish clothing is completely original, including her fringed bonnet and cape, and all underlayers. Her head is wax and her blonde hair is rooted, typical of English poured-wax dolls of this period. She has blue glass set eyes.

Parian doll, circa 1870

SIMON & HALBIG, GERMANY

ESTIMATED VALUE: $2,000–$3,000

The Simon & Halbig porcelain factory produced doll heads from the 1870s until the 1920s. The company was closely associated through much of its history with Kämmer & Reinhardt. Simon & Halbig made many innovations, including movable eyelids, and registered new patents for dolls. Their heads were sought after, and were used by a number of popular dollmakers, including Handwerck and Kammer & Reinhardt. Some Simon & Halbig dolls feature the company name or initials and/or a mold number, usually on the back of the head or neck. Hair is either molded or arranged in wigs, and eyes appear in any number of styles—painted, stationary, sleep, or flirty. Mouths can be open or closed, and some Simon & Halbig dolls feature pierced ears.

This fourteen-inch (35.5cm), swivel-headed bisque doll has molded hair and headband; her eyes are blue glass. The doll's ears are pierced, but the earrings are not original, though her period white gown and underthings are. She has a cloth body with bisque limbs, and her feet are clad in molded black slippers.

Automaton, circa 1870

MAKER UNKNOWN, GERMANY

ESTIMATED VALUE: $2,000–$3,500

This charming automaton is an exciting find because it contains its original music box, and the entire apparatus still works. The music box plays two popular songs of the day, and works on a key-wind mechanism. The doll itself has a glazed porcelain head and a cloth body with lower legs of glazed porcelain. Although the arms are exposed, they are made of cloth to allow for greater movement, as the right arm appears to "crank" the music box. The doll is dressed in all-original clothing and is in excellent condition.

Bébé, circa 1870

FRANCOIS GAULTIER, FRANCE

ESTIMATED VALUE: $4,000–$5,000 (DOLL ONLY)

A dollmaker who began making his exquisite bisque heads for French fashion dolls and bébés alike in 1860, Francois Gaultier supplied heads to numerous makers of doll bodies, including Julliens and Rabery & Dephieu. Early Gaultier doll heads have in common their pale complexions, blushed eyelids, paperweight eyes, and slightly parted lips. Gaultier bébés are among the most important, and therefore finding one even in "good" condition can be cause for celebration.

This Gaultier bébé is one such example of an exciting find. She has a swivel neck and a leather body with bisque forearms. Her blonde human-hair wig and glass paperweight eyes are typical of the Gaultier bébés, however, her size is not. At about ten inches (25.5cm) tall, she is unusually petite for a Gaultier bébé, making her quite rare and contributing significantly to the value placed on her. These dolls were known to come with their own accessories, and owners could also buy additional clothing and accessories separately.

Molded bisque doll, circa 1870

A.B.G., GERMANY

ESTIMATED VALUE: $2,000

A.B.G., which stands for Alt, Beck & Gottschalck, produced bisque child dolls and character babies from 1854 to 1930. The company is most famous for producing detailed glazed and unglazed shoulder heads (doll heads and shoulders molded as one piece), including representations of popular figures of the time such as Empress Eugenie of France and singer Jenny Lind.

This lovely example of an A.B.G. bisque doll has an exquisite face with molded and painted blonde hair and elaborate headwear. She has beautiful blue paperweight eyes. Her jointed cloth body features hands with fingers individually sewn, and she is outfitted in a costume made from antique materials, though it is not her original dress. This molded bisque doll is in excellent condition.

Breveté, 1875

BRU, FRANCE

ESTIMATED VALUE: $20,000

Brerveté is a French word meaning patented, and has become short-hand for the earliest Bru dolls. This early Bru doll has a bisque swivel head on a shoulder plate. Her blue paperweight eyes are large and clear, and were highly desired by buyers in the 1870s as well as by collectors today. This eye technique, in which three-dimensional glass eyeballs were set to protrude slightly from the sockets, gave the eyes depth and an attractive jewel-like quality. Atop the doll's head is a goat-skin wig. She has a gusseted leather body with bisque forearms. Her costume is tailored antique checkered taffeta, which accents the lovely bisque arms for which these dolls are known. The lace-edged bonnet matches her dress, which rests over her original underlayers. One of the delightful aspects of this doll is the miniature fur muff she carries.

Fashion doll, 1875
MAKER UNKNOWN, FRANCE
ESTIMATED VALUE: $5,000

This gorgeous example of a French fashion doll is in mint condition. Her bisque swivel head sits on a shoulder plate and features pale blue paperweight eyes. Her body is leather and her hands have individual leather fingers, which is typical of leather-bodied fashion dolls of this period.

Dressed in her original costume, this doll is complete with parasol, muff, and bonnet. The ornate blue silk fashion gown is elaborately pleated and features a fitted waist, a bustle, and a train. The doll carries a lamb's wool muff and a miniature fringed parasol with an ivory handle. Her wig is made from mohair.

Here, the more pronounced oval face and long cheeks of the doll are shown prominently. The faces of other Jumeau dolls are more circular in shape.

Long face doll, 1875
JUMEAU, FRANCE
ESTIMATED VALUE: $18,000–$22,000

This doll belongs to a series by the prominent French manufacturer Jumeau, renowned for the exquisite faces and fashionable clothing of its dolls. This particular series is designated "long face," for the dolls' characteristically elongated oval faces. The size 9, which measured twenty to twenty-one inches (51–53.5cm), is the smallest size in which long face dolls were made. She features a bisque socket head with paperweight eyes and a human-hair wig. The head rests on an original Jumeau composition body, which is fully jointed and has stiff wrists. Fine antique fabrics contain lead in their coloring. Over time, the lead causes the delicate silks to deteriorate, which is why many dolls of older vintages have been re-dressed. This doll's costume is period style, fashioned in rose silk. Her miniature mesh purse and parasol are also period accessories.

Smilers, late 1870s
BRU, FRANCE
ESTIMATED VALUE: $4,000—$5,000 APIECE

Jne Bru & Cie was among the most prominent bisque doll manufacturers of the late nineteenth century, and its dolls are much sought after by collectors today for their fine features and beautifully molded hands. The term "Smilers" refers to the modeling of these dolls' mouths, and the word has come to designate this type of early Bru fashion doll. Bru Smilers were not originally designed as pairs, and this pair is so special because the dolls were originally costumed as mother and daughter. Each doll has a bisque swivel head on a shoulder plate and blue paperweight eyes. Both wear wigs made from human hair. Their leather bodies are gusseted and seamed, and are complete with their original bisque forearms. Their fully original costumes include their bonnets and signed leather shoes.

Figure C bébé, circa 1875

JULES STEINER, FRANCE

ESTIMATED VALUE: $5,000–$7,000

By the mid-1870s, Jules Steiner was experimenting with a variety of jointed dolls that had both bisque parts and parts made out of other materials, such as wood or composition. It is not clear whether he produced his own bisque heads or commissioned them from another source, most likely Gaultier.

The term "figure C" refers to the model number that Steiner used to denote this particular doll; he also used other letters of the alphabet to mark his dolls. The eighteen-inch (45.5cm), figure C Steiner bébé shown here has a bisque socket head with lovely blue paperweight eyes and a closed mouth. Her body is the original composition ball-jointed model with stiff wrists. The French wig, which is arranged in long ringlets, is made from human hair. She has pierced ears and wears her original earrings and a charming vintage dress with factory leather boots that are probably original.

Bébé, 1879

SCHMITT AND FILS, FRANCE

ESTIMATED VALUE: $16,000–$20,000

Schmitt and Fils produced high-quality bébés in Paris, France, from 1854 to 1891. Bébés made by Schmitt feature pressed-bisque heads rather than ones made of poured bisque, which was a later-day technique. Faces were either round or elongated, with the wigs sometimes fashioned from lamb's wool. The doll shown here has a pressed-bisque socket head with a long face, blue paperweight eyes, and a closed mouth. She has a waist-length, antique human-hair wig, and her body is ball-jointed composition with stiff wrists and the Schmitt mark. The costume is a period-style gown in champagne-colored silk with a miniature matching parasol. Her blue-trimmed hat is in a French style typical of the period.

German child doll, 1879

KESTNER, GERMANY

ESTIMATED VALUE: $4,000–$5,000

Johann Daniel Kestner began as a button manufacturer, but turned to wooden toys and other products when a competitive button maker opened in a nearby town. At first producing only wooden, wax, and papier-mâché dolls, the company eventually added bisque dolls to the line, creating some of the most beautiful examples in the world at the time. This twenty-two-inch (56cm) closed-mouth girl doll is shown wearing her original costume, from the bonnet atop her blonde mohair wig to her undergarments to her shoes with their tiny pom-poms. Her dress is a traditional silk, a very popular fabric for doll clothing of this period. She has a traditional bisque socket head, with sleep eyes of blue glass. Her body is composition, and she has jointed legs and arms, with stiff wrists.

CHAPTER 3

1880–1889

The 1880s as a whole was a time of relative calm, but the decade was punctuated by a number of traumatic events, including the assassination of President Garfield and the Haymarket riots. Also in the 1880s, Clara Barton founded the American Red Cross, and the Statue of Liberty was gifted to the United States by France. New inventions abounded, including Edison's Kinetoscope, which forged the way for movies in the next century, and new products proliferated, including soft drinks such as Dr. Pepper and Coca-Cola. In Belgium, the first beauty contest was held, while Paris saw the official opening of the Eiffel Tower and, less publicly but perhaps no less significantly, the invention of the brassiere.

Also in France came a dramatic shift in the doll world; the rampant manufacture of fashion dolls that had characterized previous decades gave way to the newest treasure, the bébé. The 1880s mark a significant time in doll-making history, as this decade witnessed the rise of these adorable, childlike dolls, paving the way for all baby dolls to come. Bébés were made to resemble small children, for the most part between the ages of four and eight. While they were not intended as fashion dolls, bébés were generally impeccably dressed, right to their little lace petticoats.

Belton violinist, late 1880s

Bru, Jumeau, and Steiner were the chief manufacturers of bébés, and claimed the highest prestige among the producers of these dolls around the world. And competition among companies to create the most sought-after bébés turned out to be even fiercer than it had been for fashion dolls. Not only did Bru and Jumeau have to contend with one another, they also had to compete with the German doll-makers who were manufacturing their own version of a bébé. Because Germany's production of dolls had always been efficient, the number of such German child dolls manufactured at that time was significant. In fact, Germany's output of child dolls was so prodigious that it has prompted a controversy about which country actually originated the doll.

Among the German competitors ready to best the French was the firm of Kämmer & Reinhardt. Established in 1886, the company claimed to be the first to use teeth in a bisque head. They called their dolls "dolly-faced dolls," and produced them from 1886 to 1909.

The craze for automata was alive and well in the 1880s, and many famous bébés were created with special talents, courtesy of ingenious mechanical devices. Jumeau created the Bébé Phonographe, which, thanks to Thomas Edison's phonograph, could sing in three languages: French, English, and Spanish. Bru put out the Bébé Teteur, or nursing baby, which had an O-shaped opening in the mouth from which the doll could "drink" a bottle. A mechanism in the head of the doll actually sucked liquid down at the turn of a key. In 1882, Bru also patented a doll called the Sleeper, which featured eyelids that closed over the eyes when the doll was placed in a horizontal position.

Another growing trend in the 1880s was for cloth dolls, which were especially popular in the United States. While patents were issued for these as early as the late 1860s and early 1870s, fabric dolls were first produced in mass quantity in the 1880s. Parents and children alike had come to recognize the virtues of cloth dolls: they were inexpensive, easy to clean, and, because of their soft bodies, more rewarding to cuddle with.

Many of the cloth dolls produced in the 1880s in the United States were used to advertise products. They were generally not sold as complete dolls, but rather were printed or lithographed on fabric; the customer then cut, sewed, and stuffed the dolls at home. While these dolls were cherished in the 1880s, they reached new heights of popularity during the years of World War I, when the demand for low-cost items of all kinds increased.

KÄMMER & REINHARDT

❧

The doll-making firm of Kämmer & Reinhardt was established in Waltershausen, Thüringia, Germany, in 1886, by Ernst Kämmer and Franz Reinhardt. Kämmer was an accomplished designer and molder and Reinhardt a savvy salesman. Together they laid the foundation for what was to become one of the most successful doll manufacturing companies in Germany and, indeed, the world.

Kämmer & Reinhardt initially became famous for their doll bodies, buying the heads from other manufacturers. The company principals were also smart enough to realize that it is good business practice to leave to the experts what they do best, but that the operation could be much stronger if the experts all worked under one umbrella. To that end, they acquired the Handwerck Factory in 1902 after the owner, Henrich Handwerck passed away. Handwerck was famous for creating pretty dolly-faced baby and child dolls. Before acquiring Simon & Halbig in 1920, Kämmer & Reinhardt relied exclusively on this prolific producer of bisque heads for their doll heads. Putting all these companies together made Kämmer & Reinhardt one of the top producers of high-quality dolls in the world.

Kämmer & Reinhardt's biggest contribution to the doll world was its popularization of the newest trend in the early twentieth century: realism. Once the company introduced its lifelike character dolls at the Munich Exhibit in 1909, other doll manufacturers were quick to follow suit, though none could ever measure up to the Kämmer & Reinhardt character dolls.

In the tradition of the fabric doll came a new type of toy, which we now know as the stuffed animal. A German seamstress named Margarete Steiff created a small pincushion elephant out of wool felt in 1880. It became so popular in her village that she soon began mass-producing these elephants, as well as other animals. The popularity of these new plush figures would eventually lead to the design of the most beloved stuffed animal of all time, the teddy bear.

Another trend of the 1880s was to people dollhouses with small dolls. Dollhouses had always been a luxury item for the children of wealthy families, and many of these manses boasted exquisite miniature furniture, rugs, lamps, mirrors, paintings, and various other accoutrements, some of which rivaled their life-size counterparts in expense. But it was not until the 1880s that inhabitants were created to live among the miniatures. Because of their size (between 4 and 8 inches [10–20.5 cm] high), most dollhouse dolls made in this period featured mohair wigs or molded and painted hair as well as painted faces. The dolls were made either entirely from china or bisque, or had china or bisque heads with cloth bodies. Clothing was sometimes painted on, but there are examples of dollhouse dolls with removable clothing as well; accessories such as shoes were nearly always painted.

As the next decade loomed, innovations in the doll world were beginning to slow, at least temporarily. But by the end of the 1890s, composition would revolutionize doll making—and especially the American doll industry—forever.

Vermont wooden doll, circa 1880

MAKER UNVERIFIED, SPRINGFIELD, VERMONT, UNITED STATES

ESTIMATED VALUE: $900—$1,500

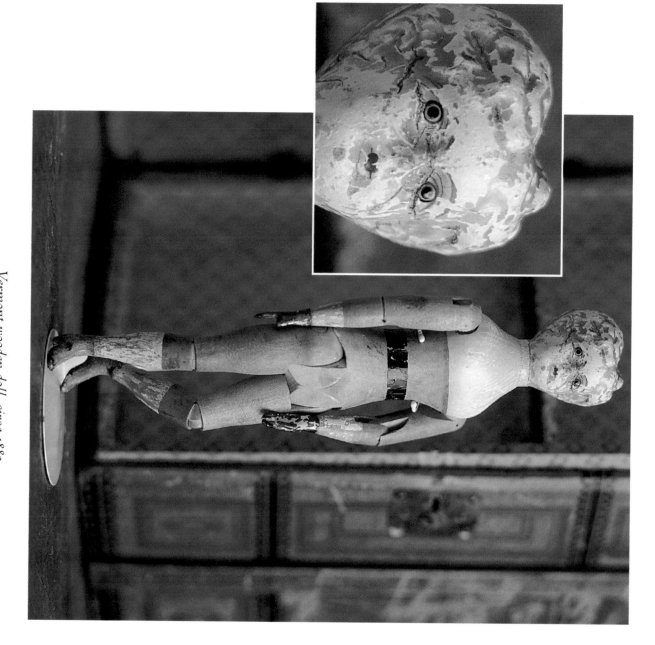

Vermont wooden dolls are characterized by their unique mortise-and-tenon construction, which allows them a full range of movement. They can swivel at the shoulders and bend at the elbows, hips, and knees. The doll can be posed in a seated position, and will hold that position without being propped up. The paper waistband on this doll makes it especially highly desirable to collectors. While the doll's body is made of wood, her hands and feet are pewter and her head is painted composition, the most commonly found head type for this body. The paint on her face and blonde hair is flaking, which is normal wear for this type of doll. These dolls weren't sold with clothing, and outfits were mostly homemade. Vermont wooden dolls were not fashionable

decorations; these dolls were meant to be played with. Despite being loved by little girls, they are generally found in one piece, which says a lot for their sturdiness.

The main attractions Vermont wooden dolls hold for collectors, however, are their simplicity and ingenuity. This type of wooden doll was produced by a number of different makers, which creates a challenge in determining the maker of a specific doll. These charming dolls were made by companies such as the Cooperative Manufacturing Company, Jointed Doll Company, and the D.M. Smith Company, all of Springfield, Vermont. Such American-manufactured dolls are rare among collectible dolls of this period.

47

Circle dot bébé, 1880s

BRU, FRANCE

ESTIMATED VALUE: $20,000

The "circle dot" designation for this doll refers to the mark on the back of the head. This distinctive dot inside a circle is one of the earliest marks of the Bru bébé. The doll shown here has a bisque socket head on a swivel plate with molded breasts. She has blue paperweight eyes, which are highly pronounced and heavily outlined, giving them a more dramatic look. The lips are slightly parted, with a suggestion of molded teeth, and atop her head is a human hair wig. She has bisque forearms, unjointed elbows, and a gusseted kid leather body. She is wearing a vintage pink cotton costume with leather shoes (not shown).

48

Kestner Bru, 1880s

KESTNER, GERMANY

ESTIMATED VALUE: $5000–$6,000

This doll type is often referred to as a Kestner "Bru" because of its similarities to Bru dolls of the decade. The Kestner child shown here has a ball-jointed composition body with a bisque head. Her arms feature stiff wrists, which are typical of the early Kestner doll bodies. This type of Kestner has completely separate ball joints as well as jointed ankles. She wears a mohair wig and her eyes are blue sleep eyes. Her open closed mouth has molded teeth and tongue, which is a desirable facial feature of dolls created in this decade. This beautiful doll's costume is all original, and is in surprisingly good condition given its delicacy and age. The dress is made of a luxurious sheer cotton, with lace insertions and silk ribbon channeling.

Bébé, circa 1885

FRANCOIS GAULTIER, FRANCE

ESTIMATED VALUE: $5,500–$6,000

Gaultier was among the most prolific makers of fashion doll heads, and also produced heads for elaborate hand toys called marottes. This Gaultier bébé has a bisque head with an antique human-hair wig. Her paperweight eyes are glass with painted lashes, and her mouth is closed. She is twenty-three inches (58.5cm) tall, and has a jointed composition body. Her gray-blue costume and bonnet are faithful re-creations, which does not detract too much from the value of the doll, as her body, face, hair, and other elements are in mint condition. Uncut antique wigs like hers are scarce. Long hair is perishable—if it was not cut by the doll's "mommy," it often breaks with age of its own weight.

50

It is unusual to come across a Simon & Halbig doll with a 740 mold number, as this number was used rather early in the company's production history, when it was making relatively few dolls. Some collectors will try to acquire an example of each mold number a company is known to have designed. The rarity of the 740 mold dolls increases their value greatly. Pictured here is a fine example with a bisque socket head with closed mouth. She has very large blue

paperweight eyes. The wig is not original to the doll, but is an antique mohair shoulder-length wig in character with the one she might have first worn. Her bisque head sits on a ball-jointed composition body. Like her original wig, her original dress has been lost, but she wears an antique embroidered dress with lace-edged collar and original white leather shoes with silver buckles. Her straw hat is covered in silk and lace.

51

German bisque doll (mold 740), late 1880s

SIMON & HALBIG, GERMANY

ESTIMATED VALUE: $4,000–$5,000

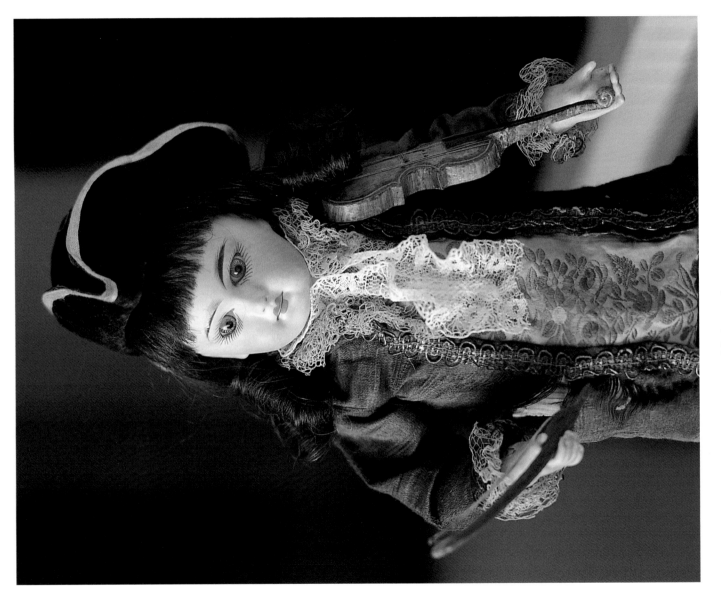

Violinist, late 1880s

BELTON (OR BELTON-TYPE), GERMANY

ESTIMATED VALUE: $2,400–$2,800

Belton is the attributed manufacturer for many solid-crowned doll heads of this period, though other dollmakers produced these types of heads, too. This little violinist's bisque head sits on a fabric body that has bisque forearms, and he has the closed mouth and paperweight eyes typical of dolls made in the 1880s. Atop his head is a French human hair replacement wig. The silk outfit he wears, which features a tri-cornered hat, is all original—including his leather slippers, embroidered vest, and lace jabeau. A music box, which plays chimes when it is squeezed, is set inside the torso of the doll. The violin and bow that he holds are true-to-scale miniatures, but while they are connected to his hands, he doesn't actually "play" the instrument—he is a musical doll rather than a mechanical one.

52

Bru Jne bébé, late 1880s

BRU, FRANCE

ESTIMATED VALUE: $18,000–$22,000

This doll is unusually small for a Bru bébé, standing only eleven inches (28cm) tall. Because this size is difficult to find, the doll is more valuable than the larger Bru bébés. Her head, shoulder plate, and forearms are bisque, while her body is the original gusseted leather, complete with its original paper label, a coup for collectors.

She has brown paperweight eyes and a closed mouth. Her ears are pierced, which is the norm for both fashion dolls and bébés. On her head is an original mohair wig and blue bow, and she wears her original sheer cotton dress with underlayers and the factory leather shoes, which are signed.

55

Lady doll, late 1880s

JUMEAU, FRANCE

ESTIMATED VALUE: $8,000–$10,000

This classic Jumeau lady doll features a bisque socket head on a ball-jointed composition lady body. Lady bodies have a more womanly shape than bébé or toddler bodies, with a slender waist, fuller hips, and a molded bust. This body type is rare for Jumeau, which means that the value of a Jumeau lady doll will be high if the doll is in good condition. The doll shown here is in excellent condition. The doll itself is a complete factory original from tip to toe, and is dressed in ivory silk with fitted waist and kid leather gloves. Finding an original costume is such fine condition is also significant, as clothing typically deteriorated over time and was often replaced. In addition to her flower-bedecked dress, this doll wears silk shoes signed in gold that match her outfit. She has blue paperweight eyes and a mohair wig.

54

Bébés: E.J. Jumeau, left, circa 1880; Tete Jumeau, right, circa 1890

JUMEAU, FRANCE

ESTIMATED VALUE: $5,000–$7,500 APIECE

Both these dolls are completely original and are dressed in their factory clothing. They have mohair wigs and ball-jointed composition bodies, as well as the original paint and varnish on their faces; both bodies are stamped "Jumeau Medallie d'Or" in blue ink. Each feature a bisque socket head with blue paperweight eyes and a closed mouth. The E.J. Jumeau doll, on the left, features original leather shoes that are signed. The designation "E.J." stands for Emile Jumeau, and represents typical Jumeau dolls of the 1880s. The Tete Jumeau,

on the right, wears an original silk dress and silk shoes signed in gold. "Tete" is the French word for head, and this designation refers to dolls created somewhat later than the E.J. Jumeau. Each doll wears the original hat designed to complement her outfit. Despite their similarities, these dolls have one main difference, which illustrates a transition in trends: the E.J. Jumeau was made with stiff wrists, which were more common in the 1880s, while the Tete Jumeau has right-jointed wrists, which rose in popularity in the 1890s.

55

CHAPTER 4

1890–1899

As the turn of the century approached, much of the world was facing growing pressures brought about by the spread of industrialization. Both nervousness and optimism about what the next century would hold reigned. In the United States, segregation was formalized for the first time when a Louisiana law mandating separate railroad cars for blacks and whites was passed. Ellis Island opened, welcoming a wave of new immigrants who would change the face of the nation. Fig Newtons, among the first commercially baked products, were introduced. The Spanish-American War began and ended within a year's time. Louis Comfort Tiffany began to design his timeless stained glass, while Marie and Pierre Curie discovered radium. Despite all the excitement in the world at large, the more rarefied world of doll designing and manufacturing remained largely the same.

At the dawn of the decade, bébés were still the most desired doll in the world. Fabric dolls continued to be popular, but bisque dolls were most sought after. Porcelain doll production remained strong, but competition between French and German manufacturers became fierce. The Germans held the lead in this contest for superiority because of their remarkably efficient manufacturing methods. German factories, such as the Armand Marseille Porcelain Factory, produced more

Heinrich Handwerck dolly doll, 1890s

quality porcelain heads and body parts during this period than any other manufacturers in the world.

French manufacturers found that they simply could not compete with the Germans any longer, so they decided to stop battling among themselves and united to form a powerful coalition. By the end of the 1890s, the two French powerhouses, Bru and Jumeau, merged with several smaller companies to create the Societe Francaise de Fabrication de Bébés et Jouets (commonly referred to as SFBJ) in a desperate effort to survive.

SFJB produced two types of dolls: the perennially popular bébés and a new type of doll, the character doll, first introduced by the German firm Kämmer & Reinhardt. These delightful dolls featured all the charm of the bébés, but had a larger span of emotion. While the traditional bébé is essentially blank-faced and seems to be staring off into the distance, character dolls may be depicted as laughing, crying, screaming, and even pouting. In the coming decades, their popularity would only grow.

Sometimes the quality of the dolls produced by SFJB left a little—or a lot—to be desired. Because the heads came from so many different factories, with molds being used at random from one doll to the next, it is not surprising that these dolls lacked the fine workmanship and uniform quality of their pre-alliance counterparts. Despite these issues, the coalition continued to thrive for many years. In fact, in 1912, SFJB had nearly three thousand workers in its employ and claimed to have produced more than five million dolls that year. SFBJ remained an active producer of dolls through the First World War.

The most significant innovation of the 1890s, however, would not really pick up momentum until late in the next decade. In 1890, Solomon D. Hoffman, Russian inventor and head of the First American Doll Factory, introduced his new formula for a material that would produce unbreakable dolls and dolls' heads. A form of composition, this special compound was registered by Hoffman with the name "Can't Break 'Em."

A mixture of sawdust, glue, wood pulp, water, and various other additives, composition cost very little to make and was easy to produce: it was mixed and then baked, forming an unbreakable compound. It seemed a natural material for dolls—and not just doll heads, but bodies, too. Despite the promise of unbreakable dolls, which would seem to give any company a clear advantage, many manufacturers were reluctant to adopt composition.

THE ARMAND MARSEILLE
PORCELAIN FACTORY

❧

Armand Marseille was quite possibly the largest manufacturer of dolls in the world from the 1800s until about 1930. Marseille was actually descended from French Huguenots who had settled in Russia, but his family was exiled in the mid 1800s. Marseille was born in 1856 in Leningrad and then traveled with his family throughout Europe before finally settling in Coburg, Germany. Although the founders' name and origin were French, the Armand Marseille Porcelain Factory was purely a German operation.

The Marseille family founded their factory in 1885. Armand showed a real genius for making bisque heads, and was soon winning awards and gaining renown in the industry. His talent for fashioning dolls paled only in comparison to his business sense, and soon the factory was buying up smaller porcelain factories. Slowly but surely, the Armand Marseille Porcelain Factory was becoming a force to reckon with.

By 1890, just a few short years after opening its doors, the Armand Marseille Porcelain Factory was the top producer of doll heads and doll parts in the world, and the company would introduce such popular named dolls as Floradora, Queen Louise, and Darling. Companies that purchased doll heads from Armand Marseille to use in their own dolls include Arranbee, Cuno & Otto Dressel, Montgomery Ward, and Louis Wolf.

One manufacturer, however, understood the potential of the material. Edward Imeson Horsman, a twenty-two-year-old office boy from New York City, established E.I. Horsman in 1865. Within a few years' time, the company became a significant contributor to the American doll manufacturing effort and would eventually prove itself a leader in the industry. Horsman experimented with composition, and in the next decade, released his famous, though unusual, Billikin doll.

Eventually, composition would become the most important invention in the doll world since the development of bisque. The material would not only carry the growing American doll industry through the First World War, it would prove to be the impetus the United States needed to become a significant force in the doll industry.

❦

Tin doll heads were made by pouring hot tin into a mold. The features of this doll, including her hair and eyes, which are looking off to one side, are molded and painted. Her hair is painted a darker color than her skin. As is the case with bisque-headed dolls of the period, black tin doll heads were quite rare. This doll has a good cloth body with leather arms and a shoulder head that does

not swivel. She wears a cotton period dress and is shown here sitting in an antique buggy of the period. Part of the appeal of this doll is that she is American-made. The United States was not a leader in the doll-making industry during this period, so dolls of this time are quite scarce and are especially attractive to collectors of American dolls.

Tin head doll, circa 1890
MINERVA, UNITED STATES
ESTIMATED VALUE: $300–$500

Eden bébé, 1890s

FLEISCHMANN AND BLOEDEL FRANCE

ESTIMATED VALUE: $2,000

The Eden bébé is a contemporary of the open-mouth Jumeau. These dolls were mass-manufactured, so the quality can vary quite dramatically, however, the doll shown here is a particularly good example of an Eden bébé. She has a bisque socket head and a ball-jointed composition body, with its original paint. She wears a brunette human hair wig Her face has circular contours, and she has paperweight eyes and an open mouth, which reveals six teeth. Her ears are pierced. She is not wearing her original costume, but has been outfitted in a rose dress patterned on a type of French drop-waist dress popular in the 1890s, with a jacket top and pleated skirt. On her head, she wears a matching ruched bonnet.

62

Walker-Talker-Kisser (mold 1039), 1890s

SIMON & HALBIG, GERMANY

ESTIMATED VALUE: $3,000

A lovely example of a Simon & Halbig mechanical doll, she "walks"—but that's not all. As she walks, her head turns from side to side, her eyes flirt left and right, and her arm moves up to her mouth as she blows kisses. While she's performing all these feats, she makes a bleating noise, meant to sound like "mama." Factory original from head to toe, she wears an elaborate dress paired with an ornate beribboned bonnet and matching slippers. She has a full mohair wig. Dolls with flirty eyes generally featured eyelashes made of fur, which in most cases has not survived.

Part of the exceptional value of this doll is that her original elements include her eyelashes. Like many German dolls, this mechanical has an open mouth with four teeth. She has a bisque head and ball-jointed composition body with a hand-operated walking mechanism built into the doll body. This is a particularly high-style example of a motion doll, and she is truly remarkable for her excellent condition, especially considering that she is a large size (twenty-two inches [59cm]). Large dolls could not be easily stored away, and so were more likely to suffer damage.

63

German child doll, 1890s

HEINRICH HANDWERCK, GERMANY

ESTIMATED VALUE: $3,000–$3,500

Heinrich Handwerck began producing dolls in 1876. With his wife, he built one of the strongest German doll manufacturers, which thrived until it closed in the 1930s. Many of Handwerck's doll heads were of his own design, but were manufactured by Simon & Halbig.

This example is an important doll with original elements that are in wonderful condition, especially because she is thirty-four inches (86.5cm) tall. Larger dolls are perishable, as they could not be stored as easily as smaller dolls. These dolls were produced in quite substantial quantities, but it is outstanding to come across an example in such elaborate and excellent condition. She has a bisque socket head with glass sleep eyes and an open mouth with four teeth. Atop her head is a remarkable original and uncut mohair wig. The original silk ribbon in her hair matches those in her dress, which is also original. She also wears original signed shoes and holds her original hat in her right hand.

Juneau commonly produced automata in this decade, but typically manufactured only the heads themselves. In fact, the company became the foremost producer of heads for automata of all manufacture. Juneau rarely made the mechanical parts of their dolls, preferring instead to buy bodies from such manufacturers as Lambert and Vichy and then construct the dolls using Juneau heads.

This doll's mechanism is housed in the pedestal and the works comprise much of her body. Her head and forearms are bisque, but her body is not finished like that of a typical doll. Essentially, her body is a mechanism covered by a dress rather than a developed attribute on its own. The music box pedestal plays a tune as the doll lifts the flowers to her nose, and her head bends to greet the flowers. Next, she picks up the mirror, looks into it, and then turns forward again. She has the typical attributes of a bébé, with blue paperweight eyes, a closed mouth, pierced ears, and an antique human hair wig. She wears her original pale pink silk and lace dress.

Automaton, 1890s
JUMEAU, FRANCE
ESTIMATED VALUE: $7,500

65

Black doll, 1890s

STEINER, FRANCE

ESTIMATED VALUE: $4,000

To produce a brown bisque doll head, the maker must fire the color into the bisque instead of painting it on. If successful, this process creates a particularly even application of color and gives the doll a gorgeous complexion that is less prone to wear or scratching than a painted-on complexion. The doll pictured here has an open mouth with four teeth and black painted eyebrows. Her ears are pierced and she has brown paperweight eyes and the original brown Steiner body, which has been signed on the hip. The doll wears a red silk re-creation with a pleated torso and a lace-edged bertha collar. Her dress was designed to match her red leather shoes, which are the originals.

The Armand Marseilles Porcelain Factory was the largest producer of bisque doll heads from the 1900s to the 1930s, and due to the massive number made, Marseilles dolls run the gamut from superior to very poor production quality. This twenty-one-inch (53.5cm) Marseilles girl doll, a classic example of a Marseilles pre-1900, is certainly at the high-quality end of the range, and is in excellent condition as well. She has lovely early elongated fingers with no wear at the tips. She has a bisque socket head and brown glass sleep eyes. Her body is ball-jointed composition and her clothing is all original. She boasts an aqua silk costume with a matching lace-trimmed hat over her blonde mohair wig.

German child doll, 1894
ARMAND MARSEILLES, GERMANY
ESTIMATED VALUE: $1,500–$2,000

CHAPTER 5

1900–1909

It was the dawn of a new century. In the first decade, Sigmund Freud published his *Interpretation of Dreams*. The Wright brothers changed the history of transportation with the first powered flight at Kitty Hawk, North Carolina. Theodore Roosevelt became the twenty-sixth president of the United States, and Queen Victoria, Great Britain's reigning monarch for more than sixty years, died at age eighty-one, marking the official end of the Victorian period.

Perhaps the first twentieth-century innovation in the doll and toy market was the teddy bear, although the identity of the bear's creator has been much debated. In 1902, Richard Steiff, nephew to famous German toymaker Margarete Steiff, designed a small stuffed mohair bear, which he debuted at the 1903 Leipzig Easter Fair in Germany. Meanwhile, back in the States, Rose and Morris Mitchom, owners of a small toy shop, created a series of bears in 1903. These bears were based on a cartoon inspired by a hunting expedition in which President Theodore Roosevelt spared the life of a bear cub. The Mitchoms wrote to the president and requested his permission to use his name for their toys—the first "Teddy Bear" was born. The success of this bear led the Mitchoms to found the Ideal Toy & Novelty Company later that same year.

Kämmer & Reinhardt Kaiser Baby, 1909

In this first decade of the twentieth century, both manufacturers and the public grew increasing fixated on dolls that were unbreakable. Durability had been no small issue throughout the history of doll making, and in the 1900s several developments occurred, including widespread use of celluloid, the advent of "indestructible dolls," and, at the end of the decade, the use of composition as the main material for dolls—at least in the United States.

German manufacturers had been using celluloid for their dolls since the 1870s, but the material was actually invented in Newark, New Jersey, by the Hyatt brothers, who had formed the Celluloid Novelty Company in 1869. In the 1880s, celluloid doll heads were patented: one in America in 1880 and one in France in 1887. It wasn't until the turn of the twentieth century, however, that dollmakers outside Germany began to use celluloid in any significant way. Within a few years, France, the United States, and veritable newcomers Holland, Poland, and Italy were producing heads fashioned from this material. Japan also joined the ranks of celluloid doll producers and by the 1920s was Germany's biggest competition.

At first, celluloid dolls were created to resemble small children—both boys and girls. But when character dolls came in vogue, celluloid became the favorite material for replicating favorite comic book, cartoon, and, eventually, film characters.

In 1904, in Roanoke, Alabama, seamstress Ella Gauntt Smith set out to create a line of indestructible dolls when the child of a neighbor brought her a bisque doll to be repaired. Because the child was visibly heartbroken, Smith determined to invent dolls that children could love as hard as they wanted without fear of breaking them. Smith unwittingly stumbled on a goldmine: in the doll factory built by her husband she produced between six and ten thousand dolls a year. These popular dolls were known as Alabama Indestructible Dolls, Alabama Babies, Roanoke Dolls, or simply Ella Smith Dolls.

Smith's indestructible doll was made using a bisque head mold that was filled with plaster and covered by stockingette—a light, stretchy cotton fabric—which was then painted. Eventually, she began to use fleece-lined fabric and heavy-duty cotton, both to cover the heads and for the dolls' bodies. In 1901, Smith received a patent for her innovative dolls, though the document was in her husband's name, and her entry won a blue ribbon at the 1904 St. Louis Exposition. She continued to improve her dolls until a bad business deal led to the end of her company in 1924.

Composition finally began to be taken seriously as a material by the end of the decade. Leading the charge was the young E.I. Horsman. After years of experimentation, Horsman began producing composition dolls by the thousands.

THE IDEAL® TOY
AND NOVELTY COMPANY

❧

Founded by Rose and Morris Mitchom, and a third partner, A. Cohn, the Ideal Toy and Novelty Company of Brooklyn, New York, was one of the pioneer producers of composition dolls. Forging their start as the professed creators of the teddy bear, Ideal went on to become one of the largest manufacturers of dolls and toys in the twentieth century.

The first composition doll introduced by Ideal was the Uneeda Biscuit Kid in 1914. He featured a cloth body and a composition head, and wore the trademark yellow raincoat and big black rain boots of the National Biscuit Company's character. Other early dolls by Ideal included an all-composition Snow White and Mortimer Snerd, which had a composition head and wooden body.

Ideal reached the pinnacle of doll production in the 1930s with their composition dolls modeled after famous book and film characters, including the Queen of Hearts, Bo Peep, Judy Garland, and Deanna Durbin. The most famous of these was Ideal's 1934 Shirley Temple doll, a composition replica of the child star.

In addition to making all their own dolls, Ideal supplied doll heads and body parts to other manufacturers, including American Character and Arranbee.

Ideal survived and prospered by changing with the times, manufacturing dolls in hard plastic and later vinyl when these materials began to replace composition. Because of Ideal's willingness to adapt to new materials and market conditions, it remained a success for years to come. The Ideal Toy and Novelty Company is now known as Ideal Toy. The company no longer produces dolls and teddy bears, choosing to focus instead on board games.

One of the most memorable of Horsman's dolls was the first composition doll he created: the 1909 Billikin, the likes of which no one had seen before. Inspired by the teddy bear craze that had begun earlier in the decade, Horsman combined a composition head of a Chinese deity with the plush body of a teddy bear and named his creation the Billikin.

In the decades that followed, Horsman produced numerous other memorable dolls, including the first Campbell's Soup Kids in 1910. These two successes, the Billiken and the Campbell's Soup Kids, sparked a composition revolution that ran through the next decade and into the 1940s, when hard plastic surpassed composition as the material of choice.

Ironically, the same decade that produced an oddity like the Billiken saw a strong trend toward realism. Dollmakers moved away from figural ideals of flawlessness, perfection, and beauty, and began to incorporate instead a sense of naturalness and authenticity. Dolls began to look more like real people, and the real people who purchased them appreciated this — as was proven by the numbers in which these dolls sold.

Munich Art Dolls, created by Marion Kaulitz around 1908, is widely credited for sparking the Puppen Reform, the name given to this movement toward realism. Kaulitz's dolls inspired Kämmer and Reinhardt, among others, to develop character dolls.

By the end of the decade, composition's position as the material of choice for dollmaking was secure and, though bisque was still widely used, its supremacy as a desirable material had passed. Character dolls and composition were well on their way to supplanting bébés and bisque.

Negre Jouant du Banjo, 1900s
GUSTAVE VICHY, FRANCE

ESTIMATED VALUE: $15,000 APIECE

Dolls created from 1862 until the early 1900s by Gustave Vichy and his sons are of the highest quality, and when they were first introduced won several awards, including Grand Prize at the Paris Exposition of 1900. Pictured here is a delightful pair of Vichy automata. It is quite rare to find both members of a pair—and particularly to find them in such excellent condition—which is one of the reasons these dolls are so desirable and valuable. When wound each of the pair plays two different classical tunes: the music boxes are housed within the stands, as are the mechanisms for some of the dolls' movements. Both dolls have glass eyes that open and close as they play their instruments. The papier-mâché bodies are jointed to allow for movement. Like many automata, these dolls were not intended as children's playthings, but rather were designed as amusements for adults, which explains, in part, how they've managed to remain in such excellent condition. From bottom to top, the dolls and stands are twenty-four inches (61cm) tall.

73

Floradora Girl, 1900s

ARMAND MARSEILLES, GERMANY

ESTIMATED VALUE: $300—$500

"Floradora Girl" was a popular term of the early twentieth century, and referred to the chorus girls of the hit musical *Floradora*. This Armand Marseilles Floradora is a perfect example of a German child doll. In fact, she typifies the German concept of a "dolly" doll, essentially a doll with a realistic but pretty child face. She is a factory original, from her mohair wig to her shoes. This Floradora Girl has a bisque shoulder head with brown sleep eyes, and an open mouth with four teeth. Her body is cloth and she has papier-mâché limbs. Child dolls such as these grew in popularity around the turn of the twentieth century, mainly because they were more accessible than French bébés, which were more expensive. German companies had long been more efficient at producing dolls than their French counterparts, in part because German dolls typically featured less elaborate detailing and simpler bodies.

74

A.B.G., short for Alt, Beck & Gottschalck, produced bisque child and character babies from 1854 to 1930. They are perhaps most famous for detailed glazed and unglazed shoulder heads. A.B.G. created a number of molds for bisque-head character babies with varying expressions. One popular feature was flirty eyes, which glanced from side to side with the aid of a counterweight inside the head.

Flirty baby, 1900s
A.B.G., GERMANY
ESTIMATED VALUE: $700–$1,000

This beautiful 24-inch (61cm) doll features a bisque socket head on a five-part composition baby body. She has the popular flirty eyes, which are a deep brown, and her original human-hair wig. Her lace-trimmed infant gown and baby bonnet are vintage. Note that the tiny stuffed lamb this baby doll carries is a charming prop, but was never sold with the doll.

Child doll, 1909

SCHOENAU & HOFFMEISTER, GERMANY

ESTIMATED VALUE: $500–$700

The Schoenau & Hoffmeister porcelain factory was established in Germany in 1901 by Arthur Schoenau and Carl Hoffmeister. By 1909, because of a dispute over whether heads should be produced as shoulder heads or socket heads, Hoffmeister left the partnership and Schoenau continued alone.

This early child doll features a bisque socket head with blue glass sleep eyes and an open mouth with four teeth, which was quite com-

mon for German dolls of the period. Her mohair wig hair is auburn, a relatively rare hair color for dolls of this vintage. She has a ball-jointed composition body, and is original from head to toe, including her lovely costume. She is wearing a delightful coat dress made of a heavyweight silk, with buttons all down the front; thoughtful details such as a lace collar, silk cuffs, and a matching bow make her outfit truly special.

Kaiser Baby (*mold 100*), 1909
KÄMMER & REINHARDT, GERMANY
ESTIMATED VALUE: $600–$800

This is the first character baby introduced by Kämmer & Reinhardt, and it was given the mold number 100 and called simply Baby. Legend has it that the Kaiser Baby was named in tribute to Kaiser Wilhelm, depicted as a baby, though it should be noted that Kämmer & Reinhardt never marketed the doll as a Kaiser Baby. This Kaiser Baby is made from a five-part composition body. The doll's head is bisque, with painted intaglio eyes and an open closed mouth. The crown of his head

is completely bisque and features painted hair instead of a conventional hair wig. He wears a homemade knit cap and trousers and a vintage wool jacket.

This doll is controversial among collectors—some find it charming, others find it homely. Note that the stuffed dog that sits in the boy's lap is not a Kämmer & Reinhardt; rather, it is an original Steiff dog, circa 1900.

77

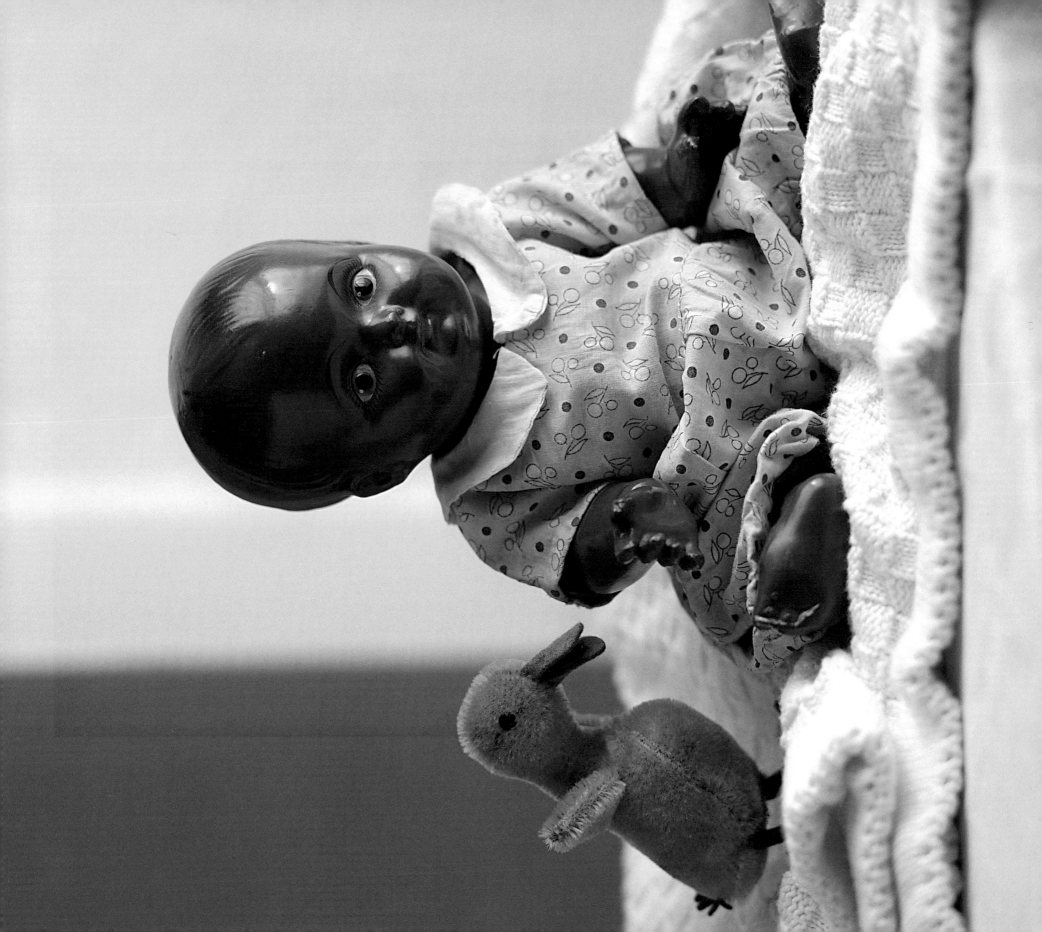

CHAPTER 6

1910–1919

I t was the decade that would see, for the first time, the entire world at war. But the 1910s began relatively quietly; in 1911, art thieves Eduardo de Valfierno and Yves Chaudron stole the *Mona Lisa* from the Louvre Museum. It did not resurface for another two years. The *Titanic* met its untimely fate in the waters off the Atlantic Ocean in 1912. Most significantly, the First World War began in 1914 with the assassination of Archduke Franz Ferdinand.

Over the five-year period that World War I was waged, the United States became a significant player in doll manufacture, partly because American makers embraced the use of composition, which was much in demand due to its durability and affordability. Germany's dollmakers were slower to respond to this trend, and their position of supremacy in the doll world slipped away, never to be fully recovered.

Especially damaging to Germany's doll industry was the fact that, during the war years, the import of German bisque dolls to several countries, including the United States and the United Kingdom, halted. The diminished number of markets that German dollmakers had access to meant decreased productivity and income.

Effanbee Brown Baby, 1918

In addition, the steady demand for bisque dolls in England and America gave manufacturers in other countries an opportunity to establish themselves, thus creating more competition for German makers. Perhaps the only thing that saved Germany's doll industry from complete ruin during and after the war was that the dolls being produced by their competitors could not compare in quality and charm to the established German bisque dolls. Still, the efforts of dollmakers in the United States, the United Kingdom, and especially Japan put extreme pressure on German manufacturers.

The financial reward for supplying the market with quality bisque dolls had become apparent, and during the 1910s Japanese manufacturers began in earnest to replicate the beautiful German bisque dolls. While the initial quality was not on a par with that of dolls produced by Germany's master craftsmen, the quality of Japanese bisque dolls improved as dollmakers gained experience.

The Monimura brothers, one of the main exporters of Japanese porcelain, were among the first of that country's businessmen to understand the opportunity created by the absence of German dolls in the market. They quickly began producing delightful bisque dolls and doll heads, which were a resounding success. In fact, their dolls were so popular that their entire product line was completely sold out for several years.

Collectors today express mixed feelings for Monimura dolls. While later examples show a sophistication in keeping with German bisque dolls, the earlier dolls are not much sought after. The main reason that modern collectors seek Monimura dolls mirrors the reason that the dolls were originally produced: German bisque dolls may soar to unattainable prices, and classic doll collectors opt for the next best thing, namely, Japanese bisque dolls that looked like German dolls.

Composition dolls, an American innovation, grew immensely in popularity in this decade, largely because they were so inexpensive to make. But the fact that American attempts at bisque dollmaking were typically unremarkable was also an important factor. Composition was an entirely new medium, one in which Americans dollmakers could set their own standards. And they did.

Character dolls remained in high demand, and several favorites made their debut in this decade. One of the most famous, the Kewpie doll, was based on artist Rosie O'Neill's cartoon characters, which first appeared in a 1909 issue of *Harper's Bazaar*. The original Kewpie dolls were made in 1912 from bisque, and were imported from Germany. Soon, though, the dolls were manufactured by a U.S. firm, the Cameo Doll Company, who experimented with every type of material, including celluloid,

A. SCHOENHUT & COMPANY

❧

Founded in 1872 by German-born Albert Schoenhut, A. Schoenhut & Company, was famous for its wooden productions. By the 1890s, Schoenhut was producing fully jointed wooden figures that were treasured by children and adults alike.

In 1902, Schoenhut created his famous Humpty Dumpty Circus, a menagerie of wooden dolls that featured various circus characters, including a ringmaster, acrobats, and a lion tamer. So popular was this collection that it led to the introduction of additional wooden characters, including several inspired by President Theodore Roosevelt's 1909 hunting expedition in Africa.

Schoenhut applied for, and received in 1911, a patent for his swivel, spring-jointed dolls. These dolls were unique in that the springs that held the joints in place were compressed rather than stretched, which meant that the dolls were sturdier and longer-lasting than previous jointed dolls.

When Albert Schoenhut died in 1912, his sons took over the business and continued producing the high-quality wooden dolls their father was so proud to create. In addition to making character dolls, the Schoenhut sons followed the trends of the day and created an all-wooden infant doll in 1913. More infants followed, including a bent-limb baby that was introduced in 1915. The company also introduced a line of cloth-bodied mama dolls, but none of their creations could compared with the high-quality wooden dolls that A. Schoenhut & Company had made so famous, even as the heyday of wooden dolls slipped past.

plaster, and rubber, in addition to bisque. Kewpies were such an enormous sensation that, between 1912 and 1920, consumers bought everything they could find that depicted these charming characters, from the dolls themselves to books, cups, cards, and more.

Another memorable type of doll produced during this period was the googly-eyed doll. Also a 1912 invention, these enchanting character dolls, which originated in Germany, featured eyes that look to one side, as well as smiling faces and chubby cheeks replete with dimples.

Newly introduced in the 1910s were boudoir dolls, also known as flapper dolls or sofa dolls. These dolls—whose purpose was purely decorative—were made for adults, and were produced in France, Italy, and the United States between 1915 and 1930. The boudoir doll, impeccably dressed in a gown, silk pantsuit, or other highly styled outfit, adorned the bed or dressing table of trendsetting women everywhere.

Fabric was a particularly important material during the years of World War 1. While fabric dolls first came into fashion at the end of the nineteenth century, they enjoyed the height of their popularity between 1910 and 1935. The main appeal of fabric dolls: simple economics. They were easy to produce, low in cost, and attainable for anyone, no matter his or her station in life.

In 1910, German dollmaker Käthe Kruse began her enterprise, designing and producing fabric dolls from her parlor in Berlin. The Käthe Kruse Doll Company, which is still in existence today, owes much of its success to Kruse's firm belief that dolls should be handmade and sturdy enough for children to play with and love. Made from waterproof, treated muslin, cotton wool, and stockingette, Kruse dolls were individually painted, and each head of hair was hand-knotted by the small staff that continued to work out of Kruse's home.

While other fabric dolls appeared in the 1910s, none was more beloved than Raggedy Ann. The design for this timeless American rag doll was created in 1915 by Johnny Gruelle, an artist, illustrator, writer, and toy designer. According to legend, the cheerful doll was based on a faceless rag doll Johnny's daughter Marcella found in her grandmother's attic. Later, Marcella fell ill from the effects of an infected smallpox vaccine, and Johnny entertained her with stories about the whimsical doll. After Marcella died of her illness, Johnny published the stories in a series of children's books, and patented his Raggedy Ann doll in 1918. Ann's brother, Andy, was introduced in 1920.

Occupational character doll, 1910
STEIFF, GERMANY
ESTIMATED VALUE: $2,000–$3,000

Margarete Steiff, renowned as the mother of stuffed toys, created her first stuffed animal, a small elephant, in 1880, and the company grew quickly. In fact, Margarete's nephew, Richard, is sometimes credited with inventing the teddy bear (though several other companies laid claim to the teddy as well). Steiff continues to produce superior toys to this day, and both vintage and new pieces are highly collectible.

In addition to its acclaimed stuffed animals, Steiff produced a variety of dolls, though these were never as popular as the animals. This little man is an occupational figure—a military officer or police-man—which was cut from a pattern, then sewn and stuffed. Steiff dolls are distinguished by the use of different costumes and different

heights: the dolls typically stand seventeen inches (43cm) tall or smaller and are made of felt. Interest and collectibility of these dolls varies with the costume. This seventeen-inch (43cm) character doll features the tell-tale seam in the fabric, which runs down the middle of the doll's face; these seams are necessary to create a three-dimensional doll. His accents are applied, and his oversized nose and ears are distinctive characteristics of these types of dolls, as are the absurdly large and pointy feet. He has shoe-button eyes and painted lips, cheeks, and hair, and his costume is part of the body. Often, the dolls came with accessories such as rifles, swords, knapsacks, or mail pouches, depending on the occupation assigned to the figure.

Each face was hand-painted, either by Ella Smith herself or by one of her assistants, lending all the Alabama Indestructible Babies unique facial expressions.

Alabama Indestructible Baby, 1910

THE ELLA SMITH DOLL COMPANY, UNITED STATES

ESTIMATED VALUE: $2,800

Ella Smith was inspired to create her famous baby after she repaired a neighboring child's broken china doll by strengthening it from within using a plaster and fiber filler. Smith then became determined to produce a line of dolls that children could love as roughly as they wanted, without worrying about them falling apart. Over several years she perfected her doll making technique, and at the height of her business, between 1904 and 1924, the Ella Smith Doll Company produced about six thousand dolls per year. In typical fashion, the Indestructible Baby shown here features a cloth body, jointed at the hips and shoulders. Like all of Ella Smith's dolls, her head is cloth over a plaster-like substance. This doll's head features an early circular seam at the top, originally a hole that allowed the head to be stuffed with cotton, and applied ears. Her features and hair were oil-painted by hand.

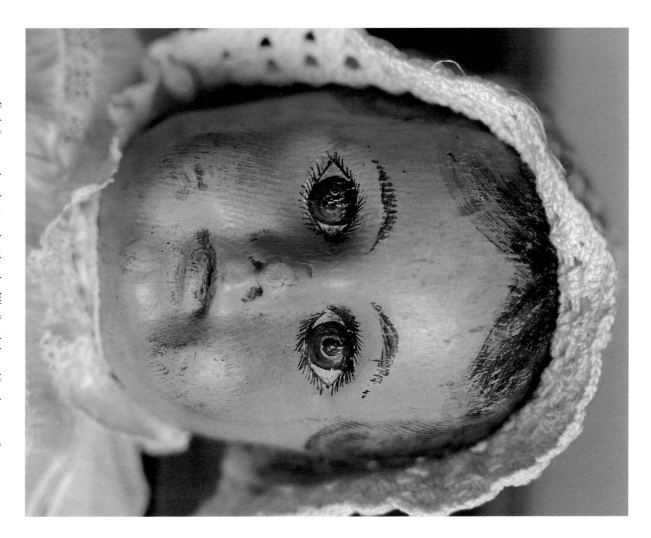

Dolly-faced bisque doll (mold 154), circa 1910

KESTNER, GERMANY

APPROXIMATE VALUE: $500–$800

Mold number 154 was Kestner's most heavily produced kid-bodied doll, and was created in sizes ranging from nine to thirty inches (23–76cm). Leather bodies on Kestner dolls bore a colorful paper label with the Kestner trademark symbol of a crown with streamers, though many of the dolls have lost these labels over time. This fine example has a bisque shoulder head, a gusseted kid leather body, and bisque forearms. She has paperweight eyes of deep brown glass and feathered brows, and her mouth is slightly open, exposing just a glimpse of upper teeth. This doll's costume and straw hat, topped off with silk flowers, are original with newer leather side-button boots. She wears a mohair wig over the original plaster pate, which is uniquely characteristic of Kestner dolls.

Hilda baby (mold 1070), 1910s

KESTNER, GERMANY

APPROXIMATE VALUE: $3,200–$3,600

Hilda is the most recognized of all the Kestner dolls, and appeared in several incarnations: bent-legged baby as well as straight-legged toddler, and these dolls could be either dome-headed or wigged. Whatever the type, Hilda was hugely popular in her day, and she continues to be prized by collectors. This sweet Hilda baby has a bisque socket head that features a solid dome crown and molded and painted hair rather than a wig. She has a five-piece Kestner baby body and her painted open mouth has two porcelain teeth. She has blue glass sleep eyes. Hilda babies are typically incised on the neck with the mold number, 1070, and often with the name Hilda. Her clothing and bonnet are factory originals.

87

Mein Leibling *character doll (117a), circa 1911*

KÄMMER & REINHARDT, GERMANY

ESTIMATED VALUE: $5,000–$7,000

Kämmer & Reinhardt introduced its first character doll in 1909, a doll designated Baby and given the mold number 100. As new character dolls were created, mold numbers were assigned in sequence. Mold numbers 117 and 117a—fondly called *Mein Liebling*, German for "my darling"—share the same facial features and represent the quintessential character child. This example features a fully marked bisque head with blue glass sleep eyes and a closed mouth. She wears an uncut wig of human hair and her jointed body is made of composition and was made specifically by Kämmer & Reinhardt. The crepe dress she wears is evocative of the period in which she was created.

Kestner Oriental Baby (mold 243), 1912

KESTNER, GERMANY

APPROXIMATE VALUE: $3,500–$5,000

In later years, Kestner became very popular for its character dolls, including a series of dolls inspired by the Orient. Doll manufacturers of the day were also inspired by Africa and other foreign lands.

This charming thirteen-inch (33cm) Kestner character doll has a five-piece composition body with an olive-tinted bisque socket head and lovely almond-shaped glass sleep eyes. He wears his original black mohair wig with queue and his original silk costume and head-dress, for which these dolls are celebrated. The completeness and elaborateness of the costume adds greatly to the value of these highly collectible dolls.

Newborn Baby, 1914–1916

LOUIS AMBERG & SON, UNITED STATES

APPROXIMATE VALUE: $400–$700

An American manufacturer of bisque and composition dolls, Louis Amberg and his son, Joshua, ran their business in New York City from 1893 until it was sold to E.I. Horsman in 1930. Before moving to New York the father and son team were based in Cincinnati, Ohio. Louis designed and produced "Lucky Bill," which bears the distinction of being first American doll to be copyrighted. When Louis Amberg decided he wanted to create a doll that resembled a two-day-old infant, he is believed to have commissioned sculptor and portrait painter Jeno Juszko to design the doll. The Newborn Baby has a bisque solid-dome head with flange neck. This doll's eyes are blue glass sleep eyes, and her blond hair is spray painted on. While her body is cloth, which made her easy for child to cradle, her hands (from the wrist) are a more realistic composition. Her gown, owner-original, is a homemade light pink dotted Swiss.

90

Part of Kämmer & Reinhardt's successful series of character dolls, the Hans and Gretchen dolls, mold number 114, are said to be modeled after Franz Reinhardt's own grandson. Both dolls were made from the same mold, and were interpreted as different genders through their wigs and clothing. These two pouty-faced dolls have painted eyes, closed mouths, and antique mohair wigs. They have

bisque socket heads on ball-jointed composition bodies. She wears lovely, beautifully made period clothes and original shoes, while he is dressed in a re-creation of a boy's suit in blue linen. Hans and Gretchen dolls were not necessarily sold in pairs, but are sometimes found that way today, as modern collectors generally like to have them as a set.

Hans and Gretchen (mold 114), 1915
KAMMER & REINHARDT, GERMANY
APPROXIMATE VALUE: $6,000–$7,500 APIECE

91

Googly-eyed infant (mold 258), 1915

ARMAND MARSEILLES, GERMANY

APPROXIMATE VALUE: $4,000–$5,000

People tend to be attracted to googly-eyed dolls because they are irresistibly impish. This Armand Marseilles googly-eyed infant has a mold number that is unlisted in any current reference book, making it a very rare and exquisite example. She has brown glass side-glancing eyes, which are also sleep eyes, and a watermelon smile, a prominent feature of googly-eyed dolls. Her bisque socket head is attached to a five-part composition baby body. Composition, as discussed previously, may be subject to damage and deterioration over time. Sometimes it is simply the result of play wear and can be readily mended. Minor body flaws on very rare dolls do not affect value. The original baby gown and added bonnet this googly-eyed infant doll wears are a very lucky find for a collector.

Baby Grumpy, 1915

EFFANBEE, UNITED STATES

ESTIMATED VALUE: $375–$425

Effanbee, short for Fleischaker & Baum, is a doll manufacturer that began producing dolls in 1910 and continues to the present day. The company introduced many beloved dolls, and earned a place in history when, in 1915, it became the first company to nationally distribute a black doll, Baby Grumpy, which was sold in both black and white versions. The Baby Grumpy dolls were produced in six sizes until 1930.

The 14-inch (35.5cm) Baby Grumpy character doll displayed here has a cloth body with a composition head and hands, however these

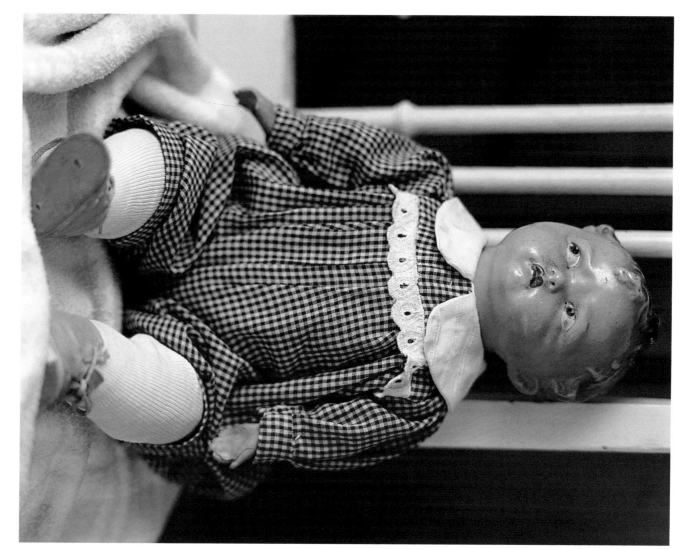

body parts show the downside of using composition as a doll-making material: crazing. While composition became the material of choice for mass marketers of dolls, especially after 1910, because it was easier to work with and cheaper to produce than bisque, it proved susceptible to damage such as crazing and chipping. The flaking on this Grumpy Baby is typical and could be worse. Her peevish-looking face has painted features, and her hair is molded and painted. The costume, a cotton gingham jumper, is typical of the era.

93

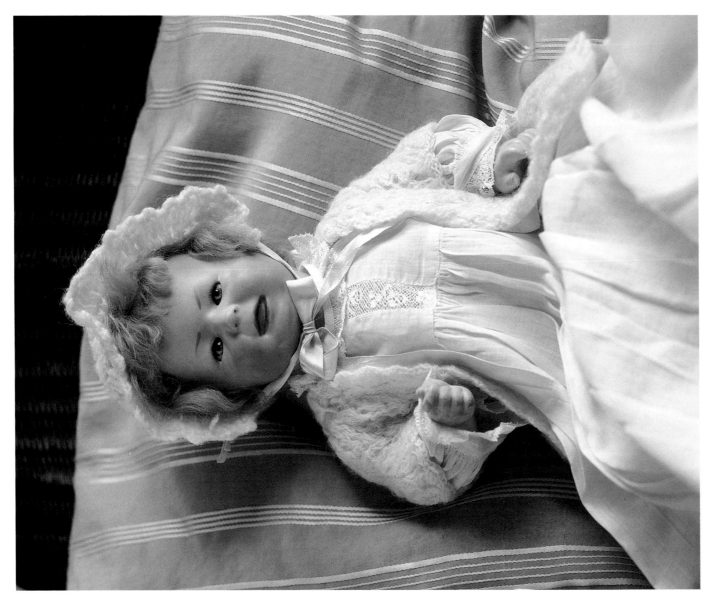

Bent-limb baby character doll (mold 1428), 1915

SIMON & HALBIG, GERMANY

ESTIMATED VALUE: $1,500–$2,000

This bent-limb baby character doll has a bisque socket head with glass sleep eyes in blue, and an open mouth. Her body is a composition, five-part example with a rounded tummy and hands meant to look like a real baby's, with one clenched fist. The doll is in impeccable condition; the bisque has withstood the test of time, with no noticeable damage to the face and no cracking, splintering, or crazing in her hands. This doll's costume, including the crocheted bonnet and bed jacket, are contemporary with the doll but not original. Her wig is made of curled antique mohair. This is a very good example of a character baby, as she has the distinguishing squinty eyes and crooked mouth, just as a real baby would, rather than the idealized features of many earlier dolls.

Brown Baby, 1918

EFFANBEE, UNITED STATES

ESTIMATED VALUE: $350–$450

Following the success of the black Baby Grumpy doll, Effanbee produced several more, including this Brown Baby character doll created in 1918. An early doll bearing the script mark, this Brown Baby has a stiff neck with jointed shoulders and hips. The beautiful, rich brown complexion was created with many layers of paint, which gives a clean, hard finish. She also has the painted eyes and closed mouth typical of early compositions. Her cotton romper is a factory piece of the same vintage as the doll.

CHAPTER 7

1920 – 1929

The 1920s were a time of both prosperity and reform in the United States. The era of Prohibition began when the Eighteenth Amendment to the U.S. Constitution went into effect, banning the manufacture, sale, and transportation of alcohol, though it was repealed by the Twenty-first Amendment a little over a decade later. Also in 1920, American women were granted the right to vote when the Nineteenth Amendment went into effect. Many innovations of the day were designed to make the chores of housewives easier and more efficiently accomplished, and included the invention of the garbage disposal, the Band-Aid, Drano, the vacuum cleaner, the pop-up toaster, and fast food, in the form of White Castle burgers. Elsewhere in the world, King Tut's tomb was unearthed and other galaxies were discovered. Art Deco, the style that would revolutionize the design world, was formally introduced at the Paris Design Exposition. But the decade would ultimately also see the stock market crash that led to the Great Depression of the 1930s.

In the decade before the crash, the doll world was thriving, especially in the United States. Composition had proven itself the best friend of American dollmakers,

Cameo Doll Company's Scootles, circa 1925

and composition dolls flooded the marketplace, becoming the top-selling dolls of this period.

The mama doll was introduced between 1915 and 1919, but it was not until the early 1920s that it became the first real American doll craze. According to a 1923 article in *Toys and Novelties* magazine, 80 percent of all requests made to doll merchants were for mama dolls. Within a few years' time, all the members of the American Manufacturers Association were producing mama dolls.

What exactly is a mama doll? Simply put, a mama doll is one that features a composition head and hands, a cloth body, and swinging legs for "walking." These dolls were intended to resemble babies of about one year of age, and said "mama" when tipped, via a voice box embedded in the cloth torso.

Among the top producers of mama dolls was the Averill Manufacturing Company, a doll concern based in New York City and run by Georgene and James Paul Averill. While the Averills have been credited with inventing the mama doll, their patent is actually for what they called "Life-Like" dolls, cloth-bodied dolls developed by Georgene, which featured composition heads and hands and swinging legs, but no voice box. Though their dolls lacked a voice box, the success of the Averills' dolls led the public to remember them as the inventors of the mama doll.

The design of the mama doll would change by the end of the 1920s, becoming slimmer than the chubby baby and young toddler form produced early in the decade, but this affected sales only minimally. The doll remained popular, but the redesign, together with the deluge of new dolls introduced at the end of the 1920s and throughout the 1930s, meant that mama dolls were out of fashion by the 1940s.

Effanbee was another pioneer of 1920s doll manufacturing, and enjoyed great success during the decade with mama dolls, as well as with other types. Originally called Fleischaker & Baum—a partnership established by Bernard E. Fleischaker and Herbert Baum in 1910—the company changed its name to Effanbee ("eff" for Fleischaker and "bee" for Baum) in 1913 to create a more easily recognizable trademark.

Effanbee was a true originator in the world of composition doll making. In 1915, it produced Baby Grumpy, which was available in both black and white versions, thus becoming the first dollmaker to distribute a black doll nationwide.

But Effanbee's most memorable doll came twelve years after Baby Grumpy's introduction. In 1927, Effanbee debuted Patsy, the first American-made doll with the proportions of a real child. Fourteen inches (35.5cm) tall and all-composition in makeup, Patsy also had smaller and larger siblings and friends.

The marketing campaign that surrounded Patsy was nearly as notable as the doll herself. Patsy boasted a full wardrobe and accessories for herself and her companions, and also had a fan club that reportedly numbered more than 275,000 members. Appealing advertisements featured the dolls "living" real lives: having tea parties and visiting with friends. Real-life characters were also brought into the act, including several "Aunt Patsys," women who toured department stores demonstrating how to play with the dolls and their accessories. Effanbee's success continued, with new dolls being introduced in later decades, including Dy-dee, the first doll to "drink" and "wet."

Another top doll manufacturer that came to prominence during this time was the Alexander Doll Company. As early as 1912, Beatrice and Rose Alexander, whose parents owned a doll hospital, began sewing doll clothes and eventually making their own cloth dolls. The earliest identifiable doll made by the Alexander Doll Company, which was officially established in the early 1920s, was a cloth Alice in Wonderland.

In 1928, the sisters trademarked the "Madame Alexander" moniker, and began producing high-quality composition dolls dressed in elaborate costumes. The costumes were integral to the dolls—and remain integral to this day—as the costumes, or an original wrist tag, are what define the individuality of the doll. Only a small number of different face types were created. These few molds were used for the thousands of different Madame Alexander personality dolls that were produced.

Madame Alexander's popularity only soared as the years went on. By the 1930s, the savvy sisters realized that the way to get ahead—and stay ahead—was to license the rights to use real stars as models for various dolls. In the decades that followed, Madame Alexander's replicas of Sonja Henie, the Dionne Quintuplets, and then-Princess Elizabeth ensured a top position in the market, which the company still enjoys to the present day.

Another favorite doll type of the 1920s was the novelty doll. The Arrow Novelty company, established in 1920, is most famous for its Skookum Indian dolls, initially made in composition and later in hard plastic. In good condition, these can range in value from $75 to $600, with composition Skookum dolls at the higher end of the scale. Ralph A. Freundlich, Inc., a later manufacturer of composition novelty dolls, produced dolls based on real people, such as General Douglas MacArthur, and on characters such as Little Red Riding Hood and Orphan Annie.

GRACE STOREY PUTNAM AND THE BYE-LO BABY

One of the most successful dolls ever made, the Bye-Lo Baby of 1923 was commissioned by New York City–based dollmaker, George Borgfeldt & Co. In the previous decade, George Borgfeldt had commissioned artist Rose O'Neill to turn her cartoon Kewpie characters into dolls. This time, Borgfeldt called upon Grace Storey Putnam, a Los Angeles–based artist, to create a baby doll the likes of which the world had never seen. Thus, the Bye-Lo Baby was born.

For inspiration, Putnam searched every local hospital to find a baby who would match her vision. She finally located a three-day-old baby to serve as a model, and set out to capture every feature of the baby in wax. The results were astonishing. When the Bye-Lo Baby was set beside its real-life model, the difference was almost indistinguishable (leading to some nasty speculation that the infant model was actually dead at the time).

When the dolls were released later that same year, store owners could not keep them in stock. The Bye-Lo Baby soon became known as the "Million Dollar Baby," because it was only a matter of months before the doll grossed that hefty sum, a pretty impressive feat by 1920s standards.

Cloth dolls remained enormously popular in this period, especially as the Great Depression loomed. Richard G. Krueger Inc. was one of the top producers of cloth dolls in the 1920s and '30s, and its repertoire included dolls based on storybook characters, as well as a wide variety of stuffed animals. In the early 1920s, Dean's Rag Book Co., a British company that had produced cloth books and toys since 1903, developed "Tru-To-Life" rag dolls, which were three-dimensional, typically with printed features.

By the time the Depression hit at the end of the 1920s, dollmakers had become very savvy at producing quality dolls that were easily made from inexpensive materials. Because leaders in the industry had explored all aspects of the market, producing dolls for a mass audience as well as for wealthy buyers, dollmakers were not as vulnerable as they might have been if they were still relying exclusively on the manufacture of expensive bisque dolls. And the next decade, despite the Depression, would see the introduction of some of the most charming dolls ever created.

Kewpie doll, 1920
ROSE O'NEILL/THE CAMEO DOLL COMPANY, UNITED STATES
ESTIMATED VALUE: $200–$300

One of the most famous and distinctive dolls of all time, Kewpie, a variation of Cupid, was designed by Rose O'Neill, who said that the imps came to her in a dream. Based on illustrations that were published in a 1909 issue of *Ladies Home Journal*, Kewpie dolls were first manufactured in 1912, and immediately became a hit. George Borgfeldt & Co. arranged for their manufacture in Germany, and by 1914 factories all over Europe were producing the dolls.

Initially made of bisque, the dolls were soon also rendered in celluloid, all-composition, composition and cloth, and eventually in rubber, hard plastic, and vinyl. Large eyes are generally painted and always side-glancing (bisque Kewpies sometimes featured glass eyes.) Hair is molded and painted. The dolls are further distinguished by their impish, molded, and painted-on grins, and by tiny wings that barely poke from their shoulder blades. Kewpies are marked at the top center of the chest with a red heart that says "Kewpie" in the middle, and some are marked "O'Neill" on the bottom of a foot.

This example, produced in the United States by the Cameo Doll Company, dates to about 1920. It is made of composition, with jointed arms and a stiff neck. The doll is molded to a wooden stand, which has its original paper label on the bottom. This Kewpie is wearing commercially prepared clothing—costumes for these dolls varied.

Bye-Lo Babies, circa 1923

GRACE STOREY PUTNAM/GEORGE BORGFELDT & CO., UNITED STATES

ESTIMATED VALUE: $500–$750

Grace Storey Putnam created the Bye-Lo Baby in 1922, purportedly modeling the realistic-looking newborn doll on a three-day-old infant she discovered in a Salvation Army Home for unwed mothers. George Borgfeldt & Co. put the dolls into production in 1923, and within one year, the doll became known as the "Million Dollar Baby" because it sold so fast that retailers literally could not keep it on their shelves.

Bye-Lo Babies were made in a range of sizes, from nine to twenty-three inches (23–58.5cm), and also appeared in tiny versions, sized between three and eight inches (7.5–20.5cm). While the tiny Bye-Los were made in all-bisque, standard-sized Bye-Los were produced with heads in a number of different materials over the years, including bisque (manufactured in Germany), composition, and celluloid. There were also some wax and wooden heads made, though these were not distributed commercially and are very rare. Typically, Bye-Lo Babies have cloth bodies with celluloid hands, though some models were created with all-composition bodies.

The cloth-bodied, bisque-head dolls shown here are eleven inches (28cm), thirteen inches (33cm), and ten inches (25.5cm), left to right. All have light brown hair that is molded and painted, and they feature blue sleep eyes. The tags on their cotton linen nightgowns (note the one with the Bye-Lo pin) indicate that the dolls are wearing their original clothing.

Bubbles, circa 1924

EFFANBEE, UNITED STATES
ESTIMATED VALUE: $400–$800

Effanbee introduced Bubbles in 1924 in an attempt to capitalize on the craze for the Bye-Lo Baby, and several Bubbles "siblings"—Dolly Bubbles, Betty Bubbles, and Charlotte Bubbles—were added later that same year. The twenty-four-inch (61cm) Bubbles doll featured here has a composition head with curved composition limbs and a stuffed cloth torso, making her more lifelike to carry. She has molded, painted hair, sleep eyes, a painted, open mouth, and charming dimples. This example is in excellent condition, with no apparent crazing on face or arms and hands. Her gown and bonnet are original and elaborate— the bonnet has a wire frame to give it shape.

Marilee, 1924
EFFANBEE, UNITED STATES
ESTIMATED VALUE: $500

Effanbee's Marilee was part of a doll "family," all introduced in 1924, that also included Alice Lee, Barbara Lee, and Betty Lee. Part of Effanbee's marketing genius was its ability to choose a doll type and create the dolls in varying sizes (the Lee series ranged from twenty to twenty-nine inches [51–73.5cm]) and with slightly modified features. These dolls have composition shoulder heads with cloth bodies and upper legs; arms and lower legs are made of composition. The bodies are jointed at the shoulders and have stitched hip joints. Eyes are glassine sleep eyes, typically blue or brown, and the mouths are molded open mouths with four upper teeth. While this series typically had human hair wigs in blonde or light brown, the dolls sometimes had hair made from mohair.

This Marilee doll measures twenty-four inches (61cm), and has brown glassine eyes with brush-like lashes and her original brown human-hair wig. Her clothing, shoes, and socks are all original.

Scootles, circa 1925
ROSE O'NEILL/CAMEO DOLL COMPANY, UNITED STATES
ESTIMATED VALUE: $900–$1,200 (LEFT); $400–$600 (RIGHT)

Scootles was designed by Rose O'Neill, creator of the Kewpie doll, and produced by the Cameo Doll Company. Scootles looked much like Kewpie dolls, but bore a closer resemblance to a real child than to a childlike imp, like the Kewpie. Scootles dolls were generally made with composition heads and five-piece jointed composition bodies featuring curved arms with starfish-shaped fingers. Some were made from bisque, but only in smaller sizes. These dolls came in a variety of sizes, from seven to twenty inches (18–51cm).

The dolls pictured here are twenty inches (51cm) and twelve inches (30.5cm) tall. They have composition bodies and heads, with molded, painted hair and painted features. Eyes are painted on, and in most Scootles dolls are side-glancing, though the larger example here features front-facing eyes. Mouths are painted watermelon mouths. While black Scootles dolls were produced, they are far rarer than white dolls and are much desired by some collectors. Both of these dolls are wearing original cotton print rompers.

Dream Baby, 1926

ARMAND MARSEILLES, GERMANY

ESTIMATED VALUE: $400

This adorable eight-and-a-half-inch (21.5cm) Armand Marseilles baby doll has a bisque dome head and a composition body. Her eyes are blue glass sleep eyes, and she has a closed mouth, which has a sweet bow shape. This baby is dressed in her original gown and bonnet. While her condition is very good, it cannot be considered excellent because the doll is slightly worn about her composition hands, which decreases her value somewhat. This doll is unusual because of its tender size and composition body. Generally, these dolls have a flange-neck head on a cloth body. The Dream Baby was as popular as the Bye-Lo Baby, and was a favorite alternative for those who found the Bye-Lo's looks too unusual.

Patsy Ann, 1928

EFFANBEE, UNITED STATES

ESTIMATED VALUE: $450–$600

Patsy was Effanbee's most famous doll, and one that gave rise to a host of Patsy "siblings," including Patsy Ann, shown here. Patsy and her companions were the first dolls with the proportions of a real child, and the first to be sold accompanied by a full wardrobe and accessories. But more than this, the Patsy dolls were the focus of an entire campaign that included promotional tours by "Aunt Patsy," a Patsy doll club, and licensed merchandise such as birthday cards, crafts kits, story books, and paper dolls. Patsy Ann was made entirely of composition, with molded painted hair and glassine sleep eyes. The bracelet she wears bears Effanbee's trademark heart charm and the company's slogan: "The Doll with the Golden Heart." Her factory original clothes and hat make her highly desirable.

Gladdie character child, circa 1929

HELEN JENSEN/GEORGE BORGFELDT & CO., UNITED STATES

ESTIMATED VALUE: $900–$1,200

Gladdie is an exceptionally expressive character doll designed by Helen Jensen of Germany and distributed by George Borgfeldt & Co. of the United States. Gladdie dolls were made in a variety of sizes, typically with biscaloid heads and cloth torsos with composition limbs. A few had bisque heads, and some small Gladdie dolls were all bisque.

The example here is twenty inches (51cm) tall with a biscaloid head and a cloth torso with composition arms and legs. The doll has an open mouth with molded teeth, blue glass sleep eyes and molded and painted blonde hair. Beneath the homemade period hooded coat is the original dotted swiss dress and matching baby bonnet.

CHAPTER 8

1930 – 1939

As the 1930s began, the United States was in economic despair brought about by the stock market crash of 1929. Although the Great Depression defined the decade, the 1930s saw many innovations, including the invention of Twinkies snack cakes, instant coffee, and Scotch tape. "The Star-Spangled Banner," written by Francis Scott Key, was declared the official national anthem of the United States. Margaret Mitchell published *Gone with the Wind* and Amelia Earhart became the first woman to fly solo across the Atlantic Ocean. In England, Edward VIII abdicated the throne to marry Wallis Warfield Simpson. And Orson Welles terrified radio listeners with his "War of the Worlds" broadcast, a tale of Martians invading the Earth.

For the majority of American dollmakers, the early 1930s denoted a period of inactivity. While doll manufacturers in Germany and Japan were finding success with the mass production of celluloid dolls, those in the United States focused their efforts on fairly conservative composition and fabric pieces. The Depression dominated the mood in the States, and, while innovations occurred every day, it wasn't until the mid-1930s that the American doll industry offered its best.

Madame Alexander McGuffey Ana, circa 1937

Franklin Delano Roosevelt was elected to the presidency in the midst of the Depression, and one of his New Deal efforts, designed to strengthen the economy, was to create the Works Progress Administration—popularly known as the WPA. The WPA provided men with jobs building hospitals, schools, and other public buildings. The WPA also created positions for people willing to be trained to do handiwork—among the projects were WPA dolls. The most famous of these were made in Milwaukee, Wisconsin, between 1936 and 1943. The Milwaukee WPA dolls were notable for the thought that went into their design and for the quality of the craftsmanship. These sturdy cloth dolls featured molded cotton heads stiffened with starch and stuffed with fabric scraps. Most of these dolls were distributed to children living in institutions, and served as tools to teach them to dress as well as playthings.

The 1930s was, however, also the golden age of Hollywood. While people commonly struggled to make ends meet, they also sought much-needed refuge in the world of film, scraping up the requisite change so they could lose themselves in the images of the silver screen. Dollmakers were quick to capitalize on this trend.

Among the manufacturers to exploit this fascination with the cinema was the Alexander Doll Company. Their impeccably dressed figures captured perfectly the splendor of Hollywood, and made stars of the day appear more accessible to their fans. Dolls were fashioned after top screen stars, including Margaret O'Brien and ice-princess-turned-movie-star Sonja Henie. Royalty also intrigued the public of the '30s, and a doll in the likeness of England's popular Princess Elizabeth joined the Madame Alexander repertoire.

Another high-profile event that Madame Alexander took advantage of was the birth of the Dionne Quintuplets. When these girls were born in Ontario, Canada, on May 28, 1934, they caused quite a stir. In the days before fertility drugs, even triplets were a most unusual occurrence. Their birth was so unusual that the girls were removed from their parents by the Ontario government and put on public display, before paying customers, at a theme park–like venue called Quintland. In 1998, the three surviving sisters sued and settled for $2.8 million from the Canadian government.

Production of Dionne Quintuplet dolls followed the girls well past infancy. The earliest dolls were marketed for the girls' first birthday. Each quint was assigned a color that distinguished her accessories: Annette was yellow; Cecile was green; Emily was lavender; Marie was blue; and Yvonne was pink. The dolls were always dressed identically; the signature colors appeared in embroidery on bibs or in other small ways, such as pins with the girls' names written on them.

MOLLY-'ES
(INTERNATIONAL DOLL COMPANY)

✧

In 1929, Marysia "Molly" Goldman founded her company, Molly-'es Doll Outfitters, siting the business in Philadelphia, Pennsylvania. The company's chief strength was beautiful costumes, which were used to outfit their own dolls or sold to other manufacturers, including E.I. Horsman, Effanbee, and Cameo.

Among Molly-'es' most outstanding achievements was their 1937 Hollywood Cinema collection, which included stunning depictions of Irene Dunne, Olivia de Havilland, and Joan Crawford, among others. Molly-'es dolls were made from composition in the 1930s, but, like most companies, they made the transition to hard plastic in the following decade.

In addition to producing gorgeous film star dolls, Molly-'es became the manufacturer and distributor of Raggedy Ann and Andy dolls during this decade, though this business deal was not without controversy. A tentative deal was struck between Molly-'es and Johnny Gruelle, creator of Raggedy Ann and Andy, but Gruelle changed his mind before the agreement could be formalized. Molly-'es began producing the dolls anyway, and Gruelle sued to stop Molly-'es' production, though not before they had created three years' worth of Raggedy Ann and Andy dolls. Despite the circumstances, most collectors revere these dolls, and consider them the most desired among the Raggedy Anns and Andys produced. And Molly-'es contributed more than a production run of dolls that became most treasured by collectors: it was this company that first gave Raggedy Ann her trademark heart patch. Molly-'es continued to make stuffed animals and doll fashions until just after World War II.

In 1934, the most famous child star of the day, and quite possibly of all time, made her breakthrough on the big screen. The Ideal Toy and Novelty Company, already known in the industry for seizing promising marketing opportunities, licensed the rights to produce an all-composition Shirley Temple doll that same year. Following the doll's tremendous success, the company produced a series of Shirley Temple dolls inspired by favorite Shirley films, including *Baby Take a Bow, The Littlest Rebel, Dimples, Curly Top, Heidi,* and more.

Other manufacturers—especially those outside the United States, where trademark issues could be tricky—were quick to pick up on the Shirley Temple phenomenon. In Germany, several makers produced Shirley Temple dolls, Armand Marseille among them. French Shirley Temple dolls were not intended for export, and therefore are very rare in the United States. One of the main manufacturers of French Shirley Temple dolls was Edouard Raynal. In Canada, the Reliable Doll Company retained the right to produce their own Shirley Temple dolls. Also, one small unlicensed Shirley look-alike was made in Japan.

Even more influential, ultimately, than Shirley Temple was another force in the film industry: Disney. Though Disney's first film, *Steamboat Willie,* starring Mickey Mouse, debuted in 1928, the characters of Walt Disney did not become popular doll subjects until the 1930s. The Alexander sisters were quick to see the potential of these characters, and secured the rights to produce dolls based on the *Three Little Pigs,* issuing them just in time for Christmas, 1933. Madame Alexander's alliance with Disney proved highly profitable for both, and the company continues to create exclusive dolls for Disney to this day. But other manufacturers—Dean's, Knickerbocker, Fun-E-Flex, and Crown among the most significant—licensed Disney characters as well, with the most popular including Snow White and the Seven Dwarfs, Pinocchio, and Dumbo.

Another innovation of this decade was Dy-dee, the first doll who could "eat" and "wet." Created by Effanbee in 1934, the Dy-dee baby doll was made from hard rubber. Later, when hard plastic was invented, her head was often made from plastic, with the body still made of hard rubber. Eventually, hard plastic replaced hard rubber for both heads and bodies. Dy-dee's modifications to materials prompted other manufacturers to follow suit.

During the 1930s, composition remained the favorite material for manufacturing dolls, but Effanbee's Dy-dee baby doll foreshadowed a future in which a sturdier material would prevail. The next decade would be the age of plastic.

Bobby Ann, 1930s
REGAL TOY COMPANY, UNITED STATES
ESTIMATED VALUE: $600–$750

Bobby Ann appears to have been inspired by the popular Effanbee Patsy, which shares similar features, including bobbed painted hair, painted eyes, and a painted closed mouth. Arranbee's Nancy and Nancy Lee, as well as numerous other child dolls of the 1930s, also follow the same model.

Bobby Ann has a composition head and a jointed composition body with molded, painted hair and painted eyes and mouth. She is a delight in her factory original carrying case, which contains several garments as well as roller skates. The doll portion of the case is barely wider than the doll.

Felt doll, 1930s

LENCI, ITALY

ESTIMATED VALUE: $1,500–$2,000

Lenci dolls were first produced in 1918 by Elena Scavini, whose nickname was Lenci, and her brother to supplement their income in the lean years after World War I. Very few collectible dolls hail from Italy, which in itself makes Lenci notable, but the company is also significant for its method of producing dolls with pressed felt, which gave the dolls greater expression. While the dolls were intended as toys, they were expensive even for their time, and many adults acquired the exquisite Lenci dolls for themselves. This is the chief reason that so many are found today in such excellent condition. Lenci costumes are much admired by collectors today, as they often provide fine examples of deco styling.

Like most Lenci dolls, this example features zigzag stitching on the back of her neck and through the tops of her arms and legs. While many Lenci dolls were made of hollow cardboard covered in felt, the dolls were sometimes stuffed. Hands have split thumbs, and generally separate fingers, though early examples may feature a "mitten" form. In typical Lenci fashion, this doll has painted eyes with two white dots in each, painted eyelashes, and eyebrows set relatively high on the forehead. Hair can be human or mohair, attached in rows or strips— this particular doll's wig is mohair. Her original costume is made from organdy with felt trim and her hat is felt.

Shirley Temple dolls, circa 1934
THE IDEAL TOY AND NOVELTY COMPANY, UNITED STATES
ESTIMATED VALUE: $1,100–$1,300 APIECE

Shirley Temple was one of the biggest stars of the 1930s, and her popularity sparked a number of doll manufacturers to capitalize on her charms, most notably the Ideal Toy and Novelty Company. Ideal owned the rights to produce the original dolls, but several manufacturers, produced lookalike versions. The doll on the left, which stands eighteen inches (46cm) tall, is a very early Shirley Temple prototype made by Ideal. Prototypes such as these were marked only inside the head—this doll's head bears the telltale paper label inside. On the right is a twenty-inch (51cm) Shirley, stamped with the Ideal name.

These Shirley Temple dolls have sleep eyes with brush-like top eyelashes and painted eyelashes underneath the eyes. The bodies are all composition, with rounded bellies, and are jointed at the neck, shoulders, and hips. Both feature open mouths with six teeth and tongue. The curly wigs are blonde mohair. The doll on the left is wearing a rare white dimity sailor dress, while the one on the right sports an equally rare plaid all-original costume, including a pin and label. There were numerous outfits created for Shirley Temple dolls, many of them miniature replicas of the dresses the child star wore in her films.

Nancy, mid-1930s
ARRANBEE, UNITED STATES
ESTIMATED VALUE: $500–$700

The Arranbee Doll Company produced high-quality composition dolls from 1922 until 1958, when it was bought by the Vogue Doll Company, however, Vogue continued using the Arranbee marked molds for several years after the takeover, until about 1960. Nancy was Arranbee's answer to the popularity of the Shirley Temple doll. She is all-composition with a jointed neck, arms, and legs. Her eyes are painted, and she has slightly wavy molded blonde hair combed to one side. Some were sold in a trunk with other outfits and accessories; this Nancy doll is complete with her original trunk and its label. The doll still has her swing tag hanging from her wrist.

THE DIONNE QUINTUPLET DOLLS

Yvonne

Annette

Emelie

Cecile

Marie

© 1936 NEA SERVICE INC.
All Rights Reserved

CHOOSE YOUR FAVORITE
ALEXANDER DOLL CO. - NEW YORK

Dionne Quintuplets, 1936

ALEXANDER DOLL COMPANY, UNITED STATES

ESTIMATED VALUE: $400—$700 APIECE

When the Dionne Quintuplets were born in Ontario, Canada, in 1934, they caused a sensation throughout the world and Madame Alexander, always attuned to media events that might translate into saleable dolls, promptly obtained an exclusive license to produce dolls in the quints' likeness. No other manufacturer was authorized to sell Dionne Quintuplet dolls, though several created sets of five dolls that were identical to each other, and a few German and Japanese dollmakers produced their own versions of Dionne Quint dolls.

These Madame Alexander Dionne Quints, produced in 1936 when the girls were two years old, feature composition heads on composi-

tion bodies jointed at the neck, shoulders, and hips. They have molded, painted hair and painted features, including side-glancing brown eyes and closed mouths. Each sister typically had costume details or accessories in her signature color—a practice not apparent in this set, though the clothing is all original. Each doll, however, is wearing a gold pin with her name on it. Various accessories were available for these darling dolls, and were often color coded to each individual doll. This set of Dionne Quintuplet dolls is complete with an original booklet about the girls and the accessories available for the dolls.

Wendy Bride, 1937

ALEXANDER DOLL COMPANY, UNITED STATES

ESTIMATED VALUE: $500

Madame Alexander's highly popular Wendy Ann mold (named for Beatrice Alexander's young granddaughter) was used for a number of dolls produced in different sizes and with various outfits from 1937 until 1948, including examples dressed as Alice in Wonderland, Fairy Queen, Ginger Rogers, and this Wendy Bride.

The fourteen-inch (35.5cm) all-composition Wendy Bride shown here is jointed at the neck, shoulders, and hips. She has lovely brown sleep eyes with synthetic eyelashes and a painted closed mouth, as well as a human-hair wig. Clear eyes are those that have not fogged with time; it's a criterion some collectors demand. This Wendy Bride's beautiful gown, which is complete with label, is original, as are her corsage and the organdy veil that flows to its full length behind her. Bride dolls are a perennially popular motif dating back to the 1860s or earlier.

Betsy Wetsy, 1937
THE IDEAL TOY AND NOVELTY COMPANY, UNITED STATES
ESTIMATED VALUE: $150–$250

The Ideal Toy and Novelty Company, founded circa 1906, was one of the most influential dollmakers for more than eighty years. In the 1930s, the company was among the largest producers of composition dolls, and had major successes with Betsy Wetsy and with its Shirley Temple doll. Betsy Wetsy remains in production, now manufactured and marketed by Mattel. Because this doll was beloved by generations and also was mass produced for so many years, it is highly collectible and yet generally affordable today. This early Betsy Wetsy has a composition head on a rubber drink-and-wet body. Beneath her knit cap she has molded, painted hair. Her eyes are blue-green sleep eyes, with eyelashes. Her mouth is a nurser mouth, designed to accommodate a bottle. Her clothing dates to the correct period but is not factory original.

Toddles Cowboy, circa 1937

VOGUE, UNITED STATES

ESTIMATED VALUE: $500

Jennie Graves' Vogue Dolls, Inc. was founded after World War I, but didn't become seriously competitive until the company introduced Ginny in 1948. Before that date, however, Vogue enjoyed modest to good success with several other dolls, including Toddles.

An eight-inch (20.5cm) doll with an all-composition body that is jointed at the neck, shoulders, and hips, Toddles was sold in any number of outfits, including this rare cowboy costume. The dolls were made in both boy and girl versions to appeal to both sexes, and other outfits included character clothing from nursery rhymes and fairy tales, as well as pirates, Indians, soldiers, brides, and fairies. This adorable Toddles Cowboy features a blonde mohair wig, beneath which he has blonde molded hair. He has blue painted side-glancing eyes with painted eyelashes and eyebrows, as well as a closed, painted mouth. His charming costume is original, and the sole of his shoe is signed. Boy dolls in this Vogue line are scarce, which makes this doll highly desirable.

McGuffey Ana, circa 1937
ALEXANDER DOLL COMPANY, UNITED STATES
ESTIMATED VALUE: $300–$400

One of the dolls made with Madame Alexander's hugely popular Princess Elizabeth head mold, McGuffey Ana was sized from thirteen inches (33cm) to as tall as twenty-four inches (61cm). The character was based on the nineteenth-century *McGuffey's Readers*, and continued Madame Alexander's tradition of selecting figures from literature and world events on which to model her dolls. This McGuffey Ana is twelve inches (30.5cm) tall and has an all-composition body, jointed at the neck, shoulders, and hips. She has blue tin lithographed sleep eyes found in the smaller size and an open mouth showing four teeth. Her brown human-hair wig is braided into two pigtails. This doll shows some signs of age, a factor offset by the numerous tagged articles of clothing that accompany her.

Princess Elizabeth, 1938

UNIS, FRANCE

ESTIMATED VALUE: $2,000

Princess Elizabeth and her sister, Margaret, were the darlings of the day, and a number of doll manufacturers, following the 1930s trend for celebrity figurals, produced dolls in the future queen's likeness. The example shown here was a product of UNIS (Union National Inter Syndicale), a designation of the Societé Francais de Fabrication de Bébés & Jouets (SFBJ). Dolls bearing the UNIS mark are generally less valuable than previous SFBJ creations, as they feature bisque of a lower quality and less intricate facial detailing. Even so, Princess Elizabeth dolls in general were wildly popular, and they continue to enchant collectors today. This example features a socket head with a jointed all-composition body. She has blue glass flirty eyes with lashes, an open mouth, and a curled human-hair wig. Her costume, which includes a delightful peach-colored dress and matching over-jacket with hat, are all original.

Butin Nose, 1938

EFFANBEE, UNITED STATES

ESTIMATED VALUE: $250 APIECE

This charming series of dolls from Effanbee features all-composition bodies, jointed at the neck, shoulders, and hips. They have molded and painted hair and painted side-facing eyes with closed, slightly smiling mouths—and, of course, their signature button noses. Butin Nose dolls were more likely to be offered as pairs (usually boy-girl pairs) than other types of dolls, though they were also sold singly. Note that the dolls themselves were identical, with the genders expressed only through the dolls' clothing. All Butin Nose dolls were eight and a half inches (21.5cm) tall, and were typically sold in assorted colorful national costumes. The costumes tended toward idealized versions of a country's native dress rather than to authentic clothing, which can make identifying the particular country with which a doll is associated somewhat difficult.

Fanny Brice as Baby Snooks, 1939

THE IDEAL TOY AND NOVELTY COMPANY, UNITED STATES

ESTIMATED VALUE: $250—$275

Fanny Brice first introduced the character Baby Snooks to the world in 1936, in the radio program *Zigfeld Follies of the Air*. By the following year, the Snooks sketches had become a regular feature on the radio variety show *Good News* and in 1940, it was the main attraction on *Maxwell House Coffee Time*. By 1944, Brice had her own radio program, *The Baby Snooks Show*, which ran without losing popularity until Brice's death in 1951.

This mint character doll version of the popular star has a composition head and hands, with wooden feet and a coiled wire body. She has molded, painted hair with a hair loop for her bow. Her eyes and open mouth are molded and painted. She wears her original costume. Originally created by Joseph Kallus, head of the Cameo Doll Company, this doll was manufactured by Ideal. Not surprisingly, she is a very popular collectible for fans of the show.

Scarlett O'Hara, circa 1939
ALEXANDER DOLL COMPANY, UNITED STATES
ESTIMATED VALUE: $500–$600 (LEFT); $800–$1,000 (RIGHT)

Continuing the company tradition of creating dolls that immortalized characters from literature, Beatrice Alexander requested permission to create a Scarlett O'Hara doll as soon as she finished reading the novel *Gone With the Wind*, two years before the classic film's release and well before Vivien Leigh was cast in the role. Given that the doll's design predates the film, the striking resemblance of Madame Alexander's Scarlett O'Hara to actress Vivien Leigh is truly amazing.

These two Scarlett O'Hara dolls date from the release of the film in 1939, when demand for the doll increased dramatically. Each doll has a composition head and an all-composition body, jointed at the neck, shoulders, and hips. They feature black wigs (black is an uncommon hair color for dolls), sleep eyes, and painted black eyelashes under the eyes. The doll on the left is eleven inches (28cm), a rare size, while the one on the right is eighteen inches (45.5cm) tall. Both wear tagged cotton garments, and the larger doll boasts hoops beneath her skirts. Clothing for Scarlett O'Hara dolls varied in print and color, and some costumes created for these dolls featured velvet bodices and hats. All the Scarlett O'Hara dolls produced used Madame Alexander's Wendy Ann head mold.

CHAPTER 9

1940—1949

The 1940s saw the United States safely out of the Great Depression, but the decade also ushered in another World War. In early 1940, construction commenced for a concentration camp at Auschwitz, presaging horrors that would affect the world for generations. President Roosevelt won an unprecedented third term in office. Staples of childhood such as Cheerios and the slinky were invented. Bugs Bunny made his official debut in the Warner Brothers' cartoon "A Wild Hare." The bikini made its American debut. And then, of course, there was the war.

The Second World War changed dramatically the economies of all nations involved. Luxuries were difficult to come by, and many necessities—from sugar, meat, and coffee to typewriters, fuel, rubber, and cars—were rationed. The severity of the rationing depended on how deeply—and for how long—the particular country had been involved in the war. The United States entered the war late, and though many items were rationed, its people endured relatively little privation. England was much harder hit; there, even clothing was strictly rationed and continued to be rationed for years after the war was over. Germany began the war with no

Dy-Dee Baby, 1948

rationing policy, but as the defeats mounted, restrictions on the use of many materials and products went into full effect.

In these years of uncertainty and outright hardship, doll manufacturing seemed relatively unimportant. In fact, very little was happening in doll making or indeed in any consumer-driven market that wasn't necessary to either basic living requirements or the war effort. Celluloid was on its way out, and—as it was during the First World War—the import of dolls from Germany, and now Japan, into the United States was frozen. Because of the war, doll production in Germany and Japan had all but ceased anyway, and celluloid production became illegal in the United States due to the highly combustible nature of the material.

But good would come from the inaccessibility, and then the banning, of celluloid, coupled with the search for new materials for the machines of war. Hard plastic—originally developed in the war years for use in airplane parts—was washable, paintable, moldable, and durable; in short, it was an ideal material for dolls. When doll manufacturing resumed in full after the war, dollmakers began experimenting with hard plastic alternatives.

Leaders in the doll industry embraced hard plastic with enthusiasm: one of the main reasons they were so willing to make this transition was that they could use the same molds for hard plastic dolls that they had used for composition dolls. And the indestructible nature of hard plastic appealed to manufacturers and consumers alike.

As with many trends of previous decades, Madame Alexander was one of the first to appreciate the potential of hard plastics. In 1946, the company released a line of Portrait Dolls rendered in hard plastic, and shortly thereafter, Madame Alexander began producing dolls in both hard plastic and composition. The Margaret (O'Brien) Face doll was a crossover doll, the first to be made in both materials. Eventually, composition gave way completely to hard plastic, which became the main material used for Madame Alexander dolls in the early 1950s.

Several doll companies were born at the dawn of the hard plastic age, and perhaps the most significant of these was Allied Imported. In addition to producing and distributing their own dolls, Allied sold to smaller doll companies. The dolls were mass produced and inexpensive, and, therefore, were quite popular—one of the most successful was their all–hard plastic teen doll.

Despite the emerging popularity of hard plastic, composition continued as the main material used for most dolls created in the 1940s, and Effanbee led the way in

DEWEES COCHRAN DOLLS

❧

One of the premier female doll designers of the early to mid-twentieth century, Dewees Cochran experienced the height of her fame when she formed an alliance with Effanbee in the late 1930s.

Already a respected artist and sculptor, Cochran had trained at the Pennsylvania Academy of Fine Arts and had studied abroad as well. In the early 1920s, Cochran met Paul Helbeck, the man she would marry in 1924. The couple moved to Europe to pursue their careers until family demands and war issues brought them back to the United States. Paul later traveled back to Europe, while Dewees remained in the States. Although they stayed married, they continued to live apart.

During the 1930s, Dewees' main doll commissions were from well-to-do families who engaged her to create lifelike composition depictions of their children. Effanbee became aware of the kinds of dolls she was making, and hired her to design a line of dolls for them. American Children dolls were introduced in 1937 and sold for $25 apiece, a sum equal to roughly $300 today.

Cochran created six different doll designs, with the idea that one of these six basic American Children dolls would resemble any child. Effanbee went on to use Cochran's designs for other doll series as well.

The war years were slow for Cochran, as for other dollmakers, and she took several jobs to make ends meet. In 1947, with the war over, she finally established her own company, Dewees Cochran Dolls. The company produced several series of dolls, including the successful "Grow Up" dolls of the early 1950s.

composition doll making. After a decade of tremendous growth in the 1930s, the company remained strong and viable through the '40s. Even during the war, Effanbee continued to create dolls, cutting costs wherever possible, but never compromising on the quality of their dolls. One creative way the company cut costs was to substitute yarn wigs in place of the standard human or animal hair ones. Effanbee's Patricia and Brother and Sister dolls of the early 1940s are solid proof that improvisations such as these did not affect the desirability of the dolls.

In the mid-1930s, Effanbee produced a line of fully jointed, all-composition dolls called Anne Shirley dolls, which were based on the main character of Lucy Maud Montgomery's book *Anne of Green Gables* and the 1934 film of the same name. In 1939, Effanbee introduced new dolls with a similar concept, called Little Lady dolls, which were essentially Anne Shirley dolls dressed in elaborate gowns. These all-composition beauties were very popular throughout the 1940s.

Some of the most charming composition dolls were made in the 1940s and the early '50s. The Monica Doll Studios Company of Hollywood, California, was one of the dollmakers that continued to produce composition dolls. Monica dolls featured composition heads and either cloth or composition bodies, but one thing sets them apart from other dolls of the day: they had rooted hair. In fact, they were the only composition dolls ever to feature rooted hair. Monica Doll Studios owner Hansi Share had patented a composition recipe that made rooting hair possible. When Monica Doll Studios introduced the first all-plastic Marion doll in 1949, it also had rooted hair. For most doll manufacturers, rooted hair would not become a reality until the mid-1950s, when vinyl gained prominence as a doll material.

For all the qualities that composition dolls offered, hard plastic dolls offered even more, and the use of composition was well on the wane by the end of the 1940s. Hard plastic was the new material of choice, and it was used almost exclusively until it was replaced by vinyl less than ten years later.

Raggedy Ann, 1940s

GEORGENE NOVELTIES, UNITED STATES

ESTIMATED VALUE: $400

Trademarked in 1915 by Johnny Gruelle, Raggedy Ann—named for two James Whitcomb Riley poems, "The Raggedy Man" and "Orphan Annie"—has been beloved by children the world over for more than eighty-five years. Over the decades, Raggedy Ann dolls have been made by a number of companies, beginning as a family enterprise and then being produced in turn by Exposition Doll & Toy Co., Molly-'es, Georgene Novelties, Knickerbocker Toy Co., and in the modern doll era by manufacturers such as Applause, Hasbro, and Playskool.

The Georgene Novelties editions of the doll, which were first produced in 1938 and spanned a quarter of a century, continued traditions set by earlier makers, including the striped legs, yarn wig, and signature printed heart. This vintage eighteen-inch (45.5cm) rag doll, dated to the 1940s, is made from fabric and is seam stitched at the elbows, shoulders, hips, and knees to create joints. She features black tin eyes set inside white circles (later dolls had plastic eyes), the characteristic four triangular lower lashes, a triangular nose, and the classic separated smile that Raggedy lovers have come to cherish. This doll's hair is made from red yarn, though over the years hair color ranged from brown to strawberry blonde to deep orange to bright red. This example is completely original and in very good condition.

Sweetie Pie, 1942
EFFANBEE, UNITED STATES
ESTIMATED VALUE: $350–$500

This charming Effanbee baby doll, also marketed under the name Baby Brite Eyes, has an all-composition body with bent arms and legs and a composition head. Originally the doll included a crier inside the body, but most of these are no longer working. Her eyes are brown sleep eyes with lashes and she has a closed mouth. A dimpled chin completes her sweet expression. The doll wears a carucul (lamb's wool) wig under a wool bonnet that features a duck head for a pom-pom. She wears a factory garment with homemade knit accessories added. At twenty inches (51cm), she's an unusual size—most Sweetie Pie dolls are smaller.

Nancy Ann Storybook Dolls, circa mid-1940s

NANCY ANN STORYBOOK DOLLS, INC., UNITED STATES

ESTIMATED VALUE: $25–$100 APIECE

Created in 1936 by Nancy Ann Abbott, Storybook Dolls have enchanted children and adults alike with their petite sizes, sweet features, and lavish costumes. Originally a dress designer, Nancy Ann Abbott began selling dolls out of her bookshop and in 1937 took on a business partner, A.L. Rowland, to handle finances and promotion. By the late '40s, the Nancy Ann Storybook Dolls were the highest-volume sellers in the American doll industry.

From 1936 to 1947, the dolls were made using bisque bodies, which were first imported from Japan, but later were produced by the company itself in Berkeley, California. From about 1948 to 1960, the dolls were made from hard plastic, and later plastic dolls are less desired by collectors. There are several characteristic features that help date Nancy Ann Storybook Dolls: early dolls tend to be chubby, while most later examples are slimmer; early ones had hip joints

and later ones had frozen legs; very early dolls are marked "Made in Japan" or "Judy Ann USA," while somewhat later bisque dolls are marked: "Storybook Doll USA" or "Storybook USA." Plastic dolls will be marked "Storybook Doll USA/Trade Mark Reg." All the dolls had arms jointed at the shoulders, and bisque dolls and some plastic ones had handpainted features.

Part of the charm of the Nancy Ann Storybook Dolls is their diminutive size, with most ranging from three and a half to seven inches (9–18cm) in height. Another undeniable element of their attractiveness is the series concept that organized the dolls: these series included Days of the Week, Months of the Year, Flower Girl, Around the World, American Girl, Seasons, All-Time Hit Parade, Storybook, and Nursery Rhyme. Because characters' costumes changed from year to year, identifying a doll of a particular series and vintage can be a challenge.

Terri Lee child doll, 1946
TERRI LEE COMPANY, UNITED STATES
ESTIMATED VALUE: $450–$500

Founded in Nebraska by Violet Gradwohl, the Terri Lee Company produced dolls from 1946 to 1958. With the help of her niece, Maxine, Violet created Terri Lee in the image of her own four-year-old daughter, with the goal of producing a companion that little girls could dress up and take with them wherever they went.

This sixteen-inch (40.5cm) Terri Lee doll, dated to 1946, has a molded composition head that features charming dimples and a hard plastic body; beginning in 1948 the dolls were made entirely of plastic. Terri Lee's eyes are painted on and she has a closed mouth. One of the most significant innovations of Terri Lee is her hair. Gradwohl obtained a patent for a doll wig made of Celanese yarn, which could be washed, brushed, and styled. This doll wears her original tagged outfit and still retains her original little fabric daisy at her wrist. As had become the trend, Terri Lee was followed by a family of dolls, including a brother, Jerri Lee (made from the Terri Lee mold, and with many outfits that matched his sister's), and a Tiny Terri and Tiny Jerri.

Dy-Dee Baby, 1948
EFFANBEE, UNITED STATES
ESTIMATED VALUE: $400–$600

First introduced in 1933, Dy-Dee Baby was a groundbreaking doll, and in its advertising Effanbee called her a "triumph of doll making.... Dy-Dee drinks water from a bottle (the only doll in the world of its kind) and then wets her diaper. Her many exclusive features make her the most popular item in dolldom." Sales of the doll would prove the advertisement to be a self-fulfilling prophecy, and Dy-Dee Baby was soon joined by a host of "family members" in different sizes, including Dy-Dee Wee, Dy-Dee-Ette, Dy-Dee-Kin, and Dy-Dee Lou, followed a bit later by Dy-Dee-Kins, Dy-Deete, Dy-Dee Jane, Dy-Dee Louise, and Dy-Dee Ellen. She would also be widely copied by others in the doll industry.

Effanbee went far in their efforts to make Dy-Dee the "Almost Human Doll," and this example, dated to 1948, included a new fea-ture. She has a "crier pacifier" that allowed the doll to cry when it was inserted in her mouth and her tummy was pressed. Like the earlier Dy-Dee Babies, she could also blow soap bubbles using an enclosed bubble pipe and her ears were designed to be cleaned with cotton swabs.

This Dy-Dee Baby is made entirely of hard rubber with a hard-rubber head and body that is jointed at the shoulders and hips. She has soft, attached rubber ears and a lamb's wool wig. Her eyes are hazel glassine sleep eyes. This example has her original pajamas, and is quite valuable because her condition is "mint in box"; her clothing, numerous accessories, and all of the original literature that came with the doll are intact and in excellent condition.

Campbell's Soup Kid, 1948

E.I. HORSMAN, UNITED STATES

ESTIMATED VALUE: $400–$500

The first Campbell's Soup Kids were introduced by E.I. Horsman in 1914, and were based on the illustrations created by Grace Drayton in 1909 for Campbell's advertising cards. Campbell's Soup Kids were wildly popular, and continued to be produced for decades, with many doll manufacturers creating knock-off versions after Horsman had success with theirs. The first Campbell's Soup Kids featured composition heads on cloth bodies with a flange neck. This mint example has an all-composition head and a jointed composition body with dimples in the knees and molded, painted hair. Her eyes are painted black and are side-glancing, and she has a closed watermelon mouth. This doll wears her original clothes. Her shoes and socks are molded and painted on.

Toni, 1949

THE IDEAL TOY AND NOVELTY COMPANY, UNITED STATES

ESTIMATED VALUE: $300–$500

Already a force in the doll industry, Ideal soared in popularity in the late 1940s and 1950s, and Toni would prove to be among the company's most successful introductions. The doll debuted just before Christmas in 1949 and went on to become the most popular doll of the 1950s. Toni embodied several innovations of the post–World War II era, including new materials and a more "interactive" component. She was made entirely of hard plastic, which was more durable than composition, resulting in a doll that could be bathed. Her nylon wig, too, repre-sented a step forward, as this hair could be washed, brushed and styled repeatedly. Finally, Toni was also packaged with a home permanent kit that included tiny curlers, papers, and a "play wave" made chiefly of sugar and water. (Dupont, the maker of nylon, and Gillette, which sold home perms, also participated in promoting the doll.)

The early hard plastic Toni doll shown here is fourteen inches (35.5cm) tall with hazel sleep eyes. She wears her original dress with label and original shoes.

Nannette, late 1940s

ARRANBEE, UNITED STATES

ESTIMATED VALUE: $400–$550

Nannette was one of the many high-quality composition and then hard plastic dolls the company produced in the late 1940s and through the 1950s. This example was made during the transitional period from composition to hard plastic, and is all composition. She wears a tagged costume intended for the hard plastic dolls—most likely, she represents previous doll inventory outfitted in the newer clothing. Beneath the gabardine coat and hat is her original scarlet cotton all-in-one. She has brown glassine eyes with lashes and a closed mouth. Of late, dolls like Nannette are being referred to as fashion dolls, because they typify the styles of their era.

Margaret Rose, circa 1949

ALEXANDER DOLL COMPANY, UNITED STATES

ESTIMATED VALUE: $600–$800

Margaret Rose is the doll fashioned by Madame Alexander to represent the younger sister of then-Princess Elizabeth. The Margaret Rose mold was used for several later Madame Alexander dolls, including Margaret O'Brien, Karen the Ballerina, Alice in Wonderland, and Hulda, a black doll. In 1953, the mold was even used for a Princess Elizabeth doll.

Early Margaret Rose dolls were made of composition, but this version, which dates to about 1949, is made of hard plastic, a newly introduced doll material at that time. She has green-gray sleep eyes with dark pupils and rims, a blonde curled mohair wig, a painted closed mouth, and the highly desirable sun-tanned complexion. This example is factory dressed with label.

CHAPTER 10

1950–1960

The 1950s mark the end of the classic doll era. In the world at large, the sales of television sets rocketed, reaching 60,000 per week by 1950. But the television age would not begin in earnest the debut of NBC's groundbreaking *Your Show of Shows*. Also changing the world in this decade: the release of Elvis Presley's first album in 1956 and the debut of American Bandstand that same year. The modern age had begun.

It was also wartime again. The United States joined South Korea in their fight against North Korean aggression. Elizabeth II became the reigning monarch of Great Britain, and Dwight D. Eisenhower succeeded Harry S. Truman as president of the United States. Rosa Parks' refusal to move to the back of the bus launched the Civil Rights Movement.

In the 1950s, much of the world was enjoying an era of post-war prosperity. The suburb was the neighborhood of choice in the United States. The ideal American family unit was widely depicted on television and held up as a desirable model for families everywhere. And the new medium of television spawned a whole new way of

Little Miss Revlon, late 1950s

advertising. Products were efficiently aimed directly at children, as images of toys interrupted their Saturday morning cartoons. Mattel had been advertising on the *Mickey Mouse Club* since its first year in 1955, and other companies soon followed suit.

These scores of ads touted dolls and toys made of that new wonder material, hard plastic, which had revolutionized the doll industry by making production easier and more cost-effective than ever before. The 1950s, a decade of optimism and affluence, saw the introduction of dozens of new dolls, more than in any previous decade. While the sheer volume of dolls produced renders it impossible to discuss them all, we'll touch on the highlights.

Vogue Dolls, Inc.—established by Jennie H. Graves in her Sommerville, Massachusetts, home—was originally a producer of doll clothing exclusively. In the 1930s, however, Graves decided to introduce her own dolls. She used undressed bisque dolls made by such revered German manufacturers as Armand Marseille and Kämmer & Reinhardt and dressed them in her own fashions: thus, the first Vogue Dolls were born. Graves began modestly, but her production would soar when her famous Ginny doll was introduced in 1949.

From her inception, Ginny was an undeniable success. Eventually named for Graves' daughter, Virginia, Ginny dolls initially carried a number of different names, including Carol, Lucy, and Tina, before officially receiving the name Ginny in 1951. Even before the hard plastic Ginny, a composition doll named Toddles was essentially the same type of doll, though Toddles never garnered the attention that Ginny did.

The sprightly, eight-inch (20.5cm) -tall Ginny had blue or brown eyes with painted-on lashes. By the mid 1950s, she featured a head that could turn and she could also walk.

Like Effanbee's Patsy of the 1920s or Mattel's Barbie of the late 1950s, successful dolls required companions. So, by the mid 1950s, Ginny had an entire family of siblings, including two brothers and two sisters.

Ginny's success continued throughout the '50s and for many years to follow, and she also sparked a trend of similar dolls that were the predecessors of the Barbie doll. In the mid to late 1950s, Cosmopolitan created 7½-inch (19cm) Ginger dolls, which were considerably less expensive but more colorful and durable than Ginny. The Terri Lee Company, founded in 1946, produced ten- to sixteen-inch (25.5–40.5cm) "Ginny type" dolls and a whole circle of friends to go along with them.

Ideal's largest—though not their only—contribution to the decade were the fashion dolls Toni and Little Miss Revlon.

THE FASHION DOLL
THAT CHANGED THE WORLD

⚘

Though this book focuses on classic rather than modern dolls, we cannot fail to mention Barbie, the most popular doll of the twentieth century, who made her debut in 1959. Barbie's story really begins with Ruth Mosko, who in high school met the man she was to marry, Elliot Handler. No ordinary couple, the Handlers started their toy company with partner Harold Matson, in 1945. Taking the "Mat" from Matson and the "Ell," from Elliot, they named their new company Mattel. The following year Matson became ill, so the Handlers bought him out but kept the name.

Ruth, however, was the partner responsible for creating one of the most important dolls of the twentieth century. The parents of two young children, the Handlers took inspiration for their toys from their own children: they observed carefully the things their children liked to play with. In the mid 1950s, the Handlers' daughter, Barbara, spent most of her time playing mommy to a series of baby dolls. But what impressed Ruth most was the amount of time little Barbara spent dressing her one-dimensional paper dolls in various fashions.

It occurred to Ruth that there weren't any fashion dolls being made for children to play with, with the exception of Miss Revlon, who essentially had a child's body paired with an adult face. In Gemany, a popular twelve-inch (30.5cm) doll based on an adult comic strip, Bild Lili, was sold with her own fashions. Ruth decided that it was time for an American version of this doll, but it took years for her to convince the board of directors that the time was right for a true fashion doll, one with an adult body and sophisticated clothes. She finally won them over, and the Barbie doll, named for Barbara Handler, was born. The doll made her debut in 1959 and that year more than 350,000 Barbie dolls were sold—a new record for the doll world.

Television's lure was reflected in the doll industry, and the new medium began a trend for dolls in the image of stars of the small screen. In 1955, the Baby Barry Toy Co. of New York put out an Emmett Kelly as Willie the Clown vinyl doll. Mouseketeers from the popular Disney show were soon rendered in vinyl. Cosmopolitan's Ginger dolls were among the cutest examples of dressed-up mouseketeer dolls. The popularity of Westerns saw many dolls created in that vein, including a 1950s Davy Crockett doll by Vogue and various cowboy, cowgirl, and Indian characters from Allied Grand Doll Manufacturing Inc.

Established in 1945, Mattel swiftly became one of the top doll producers of the 1950s and beyond. Ruth Handler's vision and marketing savvy set a standard that toy manufacturers are still attempting to match. The two most famous dolls released by Mattel in the late 1950s, Chatty Cathy and Barbie, are favorites even today. The Mattel company would go on to produce such favorite toys as Cabbage Patch Kids and Hot Wheels and Matchbox cars.

Little Women, early 1950s

ALEXANDER DOLL COMPANY

ESTIMATED VALUE: $500 APIECE

Little Women, Louisa May Alcott's timeless classic, was Madame Alexander's favorite book as a child, and she first introduced cloth dolls based on the characters to coincide with the release of the 1933 film. The series proved popular with children and collectors alike, and over the years Madame Alexander re-issued Little Women dolls, with variations in size, material, coloring, and costume. Costumes are generally cotton with organdy or dotted swiss accents. The delightful dolls shown here were produced by Madame Alexander in the likenesses of the March women: (left to right) Beth, Marme, Jo, Meg, and Amy. This set was inspired by the 1949 version of the film, which starred June Allyson, Margaret O'Brien, Elizabeth Taylor, Janet Leigh, and Mary Astor. These fourteen-inch (35.5cm) dolls were made entirely of hard plastic, and feature synthetic wigs and glassine sleep eyes with synthetic lashes These five dolls use only two different face molds— the Maggie face and the Margaret face—with the personalities defined by their costumes, a popular device of Madame Alexander's.

Margaret face Babs Skater, circa 1950 (left); Maggie face doll, circa 1950 (right)

ALEXANDER DOLL COMPANY, UNITED STATES

ESTIMATED VALUE: $800 (LEFT); $600 (RIGHT)

The Margaret face dolls were based on a mold created in the image of child actress Margaret O'Brien. While the first Margaret face dolls were made of composition, they were later rendered in hard plastic. This thirteen-inch (45.5cm) Babs Skater is made entirely of hard plastic, and is jointed at the neck, shoulders, and hips. She has brown oval sleep eyes with synthetic lashes, a slightly smiling mouth, and a human-hair wig. These dolls were available in several different skating outfits, including the velvet dress Babs wears here, which probably had a matching cap. The Margaret face mold was used for many later Madame Alexander dolls, including Snow White, Cinderella, Peter Pan, and Little Women.

Compared with the Margaret face, the Maggie face has chubbier cheeks and a more circular shape, with sleep eyes that are often described as "owlish" in their roundness. The doll shown here is seventeen inches (43cm) tall, and is made entirely of hard plastic, jointed at the neck, shoulders, and hips. She has single-stroke eyebrows painted high on the face and a closed, unsmiling mouth. Her wig is blonde floss and she wears a cotton floral print dress with puffed sleeves. Note that the poodle she holds is a period accessory, and was not marketed with the doll. Like the Margaret face mold, the mold for this doll was used for a number of later Madame Alexander dolls, including Kathy, Alice in Wonderland, Betty, and Glamour Girls.

Saucy Walker, circa 1951

IDEAL TOY AND NOVELTY COMPANY, UNITED STATES

ESTIMATED VALUE: $125—$200

Introduced in 1951 by Ideal, Saucy is a popular and accessible collectible doll today, especially prized by those who remember her fondly from childhood. In 1952 Saucy was joined by a Saucy boy walker, and the family grew to accommodate a toddler (1953) and a big sister (1954). The doll shown here is a twenty-two-inch (56cm) straight-leg walker made entirely of hard plastic, jointed at the neck, shoulders, and hips.

Her torso encloses a crier and features holes in the hard plastic to better allow the sound to escape. As she walks, she turns her head from side to side. She has a round face with flirty sleep eyes with eyelashes and small arched painted eyebrows. Her braided hair is synthetic and rooted. She has an open mouth with two upper teeth. Her dress is original.

Honey, circa 1952

EFFANBEE, UNITED STATES

ESTIMATED VALUE: $350

Honey was one of the most popular dolls of the 1950s, and sparked a very successful series, which included a Cinderella and Prince Charming set as well as ice skaters, ballerinas, brides, and storybook characters, among many others. This adorable fourteen-inch (35.5cm) Honey doll is made entirely of hard plastic, and is jointed at the neck, shoulders, and hips. She has a plump-cheeked face with lovely ice-blue sleep eyes, synthetic lashes, and a synthetic platinum rooted wig. Honey is wearing her original organdy dress with pink flowers and her original hat. Her closed, painted mouth is unsmiling but not unhappy.

Ginny, 1954

VOGUE DOLLS, UNITED STATES

ESTIMATED VALUE: $500–$600

Vogue founder Jennie Graves began her business by dressing bisque dolls made by Kämmer & Reinhardt and others, but soon found that the demand for her fashions warranted her own dolls. She had some modest successes in the 1930s with composition dolls, most notably Toddles, but her crowning achievement was Ginny. Named for Jennie's eldest daughter, Virginia, Ginny was the original hard plastic miniature doll. Early Ginny dolls typically had brown or blue sleep eyes with painted eyelashes; molded lashes were added in 1955.

This eight-inch (20.5cm) straight-leg walker, introduced in 1954, is all-original, with her factory packaging and literature intact. This example has blue sleep eyes and a blonde synthetic wig arranged in braided pigtails. She wears a correct Ginny ensemble, which the original owner bought separately (this doll came undressed, as her box attests)—there were many Ginny outfits and accessories from which to choose. The mint-in-box distinction gives this example heightened value.

Toni Walker, 1954
THE IDEAL TOY AND NOVELTY COMPANY
ESTIMATED VALUE: $450–$650

Toni is an Ideal doll, first introduced in 1949, that achieved great popularity in the mass market. The Toni Walker followed up on the remarkable success of the original Toni doll, adding a walking feature, which many little girls of the time found exciting. Perhaps the favorite aspect of Toni, both the original and the walker version, was her stylable hair. In fact, miniature curlers, a "home permanent" solution called a Play Wave, and tiny curling papers sometimes came with the doll. This hard plastic Toni Walker is in her original box and still has her original swing tag. She has sleep eyes with lashes, a closed mouth, and lovely coloring with a nylon wig in brunette, a very unusual color. Her organdy dress is original, as are her shoes, one of which has discolored over time.

Ginger, 1955
COSMOPOLITAN, UNITED STATES
ESTIMATED VALUE: $325–475

Ginger was the brainchild of a former Vogue sales representative, who understood firsthand the sales potential of Ginny-type dolls and in 1954 founded her own company, Cosmopolitan, to compete in the same market. Ginger, also made from hard plastic, was considerably less expensive than Ginny. The very first Ginger dolls had painted eyes, then had large eyes with painted lashes.

This example, which most likely dates to 1955, features a jointed hard plastic body, long blonde saran wig, and smaller eyes than the earlier dolls. These are blue sleep eyes with synthetic eyelashes and the finely painted eyebrows and dimpled chin that characterize the Ginger dolls. Her mouth is molded closed and painted. She wears her original canary yellow costume.

Little Miss Revlon, late 1950s
IDEAL TOY AND NOVELTY COMPANY
ESTIMATED VALUE: $200–$300

Precursor to the perennially popular Barbie doll, the ten-and-a-half-inch (26.5cm) Little Miss Revlon was created by Ideal in response to a market that was becoming saturated with baby dolls and was craving the fashion dolls popular in decades past. Earlier Miss Revlon dolls were larger—fifteen to twenty-three inches (38–58.5cm)—and were created as a tie-in with Revlon cosmetics. Little Miss Revlons were easier to dress, but featured the same made-up adult faces as their larger sisters. The doll featured an extensive wardrobe and came with a girdle and bra. She had high heel shoes and typically was sold with earrings, many of which have unfortunately discolored the vinyl of the dolls' ears over time.

This example has a vinyl head with a solid vinyl body, jointed at the neck, shoulders, waist, and hips. She has rooted synthetic blonde hair intended to be worn in a pony-tail, described on original boxes as "pony-tail blond." Her blue eyes are sleep eyes with synthetic eyelashes, and she has a closed, painted, unsmiling mouth. Her ears are pierced and she has painted finger- and toenails—the first doll to do so. Little Miss Revlon is featured here with her original trunk and wardrobe. The gown she is wearing was a promotional tie-in with Kellogg's cereal, and was offered by mail-order, along with other garments. A larger example of the same trunk is marked "Cass Toys, Made in New England, Showrooms 200 Fifth Avenue, New York City."

Tiny Tears, late 1950s
AMERICAN CHARACTER, UNITED STATES
ESTIMATED VALUE: $150–$225

Also known as the American Doll and Toy Corporation, the American Character doll company began operation in 1919 and produced American-made dolls and doll heads until 1968. Over the years, the company introduced a number of beloved dolls, including Sweet Sue, Betsy McCall, and of course, Tiny Tears. First introduced in 1950, the earliest Tiny Tears dolls were made with hard plastic heads and rubber bodies, but the rubber unfortunately tends to crack and degrade. Later dolls were made with vinyl heads and rubber bodies or all in vinyl. Many of the later Tiny Tears also featured "rock-a-bye" eyes, which allowed the doll to be laid down with her eyes open; the eyes would slowly close as the doll was rocked "to sleep."

This Tiny Tears doll, dated to the late 1950s, has an all-vinyl head with rooted saran hair in the rare brunette color and a vinyl body, jointed at the neck, shoulders, and hips. She has blue rock-a-bye eyes with synthetic lashes, a nurser mouth, and tiny ducts at the eyes that cried real tears. Like Betsy Wetsy, Tiny Tears also came with a bottle and a bubble pipe, from which she could blow bubbles when her tummy was squeezed. Tiny Tears was marketed with a full range of accessories sold separately, including a Tiny Tears logo cradle, tub and monogrammed towel, high chair, stroller, and complete layette. This example has her original bunting and the accessories that came with the doll in the bunting pockets.

GLOSSARY

All-bisque: Doll made entirely of bisque—head and body.

Applied ears: Ears applied to doll after the mold for the head has been poured.

Articulation: The jointing of a doll.

Ball-jointed: A type of joint that makes use of a wooden ball in the socket, which provides greater movement.

Bébé: Late-nineteenth-century French bisque dolls made to represent small children.

Bent-limb body: Five-piece body with curved arms and legs, jointed at shoulders and hips.

Bisque: Unglazed porcelain.

Book value: A doll's value as found in a price guide; not necessarily the price for which you can expect to buy or sell a doll. Actual pricing varies considerably with condition, provenance, rarity, and other factors.

Breveté: French word for patented, sometimes abbreviated to Bte. or B.T.E. Has also come to represent a type of early Bru doll.

Caracurl: Karakul lamb's pelt, used to make dolls' wigs.

Celluloid: An early plastic used to make dolls; was discontinued in part because of its flammability.

Character doll: Doll made to look like a realistic infant, child, or adult rather than stylized, like most early dolls.

China: Glazed porcelain.

Closed mouth: Sculpted mouth that is closed, with no teeth showing.

Composition: A mixture made mainly of wood pulp, sawdust, and glue, used to make dolls.

Crazing: A network of fine cracks that develops on painted surface of composition dolls, and sometimes on china ones as well.

DEP: Mark often found on French and German dolls; an abbreviation for the French word *déposé*, meaning "registered."

Dolly face: A term used by German makers to denote an idealized child face, typically rounded and with an open mouth.

Domed head: Also known as a "Belton head"; a doll's head with a closed or domed top.

D.R.G.M.: German marking indicating a registered design.

Fashion doll: A French or German bisque-headed lady doll made in the mid to late nineteenth century.

Feathered brows: Eyebrows that are painted with many tiny strokes.

Five-piece body: A body composed of torso, arms, and legs.

Fixed eyes: Eyes that are set in a stationary position.

Flange neck: Doll's neck with ridge and holes at the base for attaching to a cloth body.

Flirty eyes: Doll's eyes that move from side to side.

Flocked hair: Short fibers glued to a doll's head to represent hair.

GES: Abbreviation for *gesch*, the German word for patent.

Googly eyes: Large, round eyes that look to the side.

Gusseted joint: A joint sewn into cloth or leather doll bodies, which gives the doll movement at the joint.

Hairline: Type of crack found in bisque dolls; hairline cracks may significantly affect value.

Hard plastic: Durable plastic used to make dolls after World War II.

Intaglio eyes: Eyes that are molded into the head and then painted.

Inset eyes: Unmovable eyes set into a doll's head.

Kid: Soft leather made from lambs or young goats.

Lady doll: A doll made to represent an adult woman's figure.

Mama doll: A doll intended to resemble a baby of about one year of age, usually with composition head and hands, a cloth body, and swinging legs for walking. These dolls said "mama" from a voice box embedded in the cloth torso.

Mask face: A stiff face that covers only the front of a doll's head.

Mohair: Angora goat hair used for antique doll wigs.

Molded ears: Ears molded with the doll's head.

Open mouth: Mouth molded with lips open to reveal teeth or tongue.

Open closed mouth: Mouth molded to appear open, but with no opening in the bisque.

Open head: Doll head with cut crown where eyes are inserted; the top of the head is covered by a pate, often made of cork.

Original costume: Clothing that was first made for the doll, either factory- or producer-made, or (as is the case with many older dolls) made at home by the owner of the doll.

Painted eyes: Eyes that have been painted on.

Paperweight eyes: Glass eyes that protrude a bit, giving the eyes an appearance of great depth.

Parian: Doll made of untinted bisque.

Pate: Cardboard, cork, or other material that covers the crown in an open-head doll.

Personality doll: Doll molded in the image of a famous person.

Portrait doll: A late 1800s and early 1900s bisque doll made to represent a person.

Poupeé de Mode: Term used for French fashion dolls.

Rub: A spot where color has worn away.

Shoulder head: Doll's head and shoulders that are molded together in one piece.

Shoulder plate: The shoulder portion of a shoulder head. Also, the bisque shoulders used with a swivel head.

Sleep eyes: Dolls' eyes that close when the doll is laid down.

Socket head: Doll's head molded with a neck that is placed into the doll's body.

Solid dome: Head with no crown opening.

Stockinette: Soft, stretchy, jersey fabric used for making dolls.

Swivel head: Socket head that uses separate shoulder plates.

Turned head: Shoulder head with head turned slightly.

Vinyl: Plastic developed in the mid 1950s that became the dominant type of plastic used to make dolls from that time; it can be hard or soft.

Voice box: Mechanism in a doll's body that allows the doll to make sound.

Watermelon mouth: A closed, smiling mouth.

Weighted eyes: Sleep eyes operated by a weight attached to the wire frame that holds the eye in place.

MAGAZINES

Antique Doll Collector
www.tias.com/mags/adc
adc@tias.com
6 Woodside Avenue, Suite 300
Northport, NY 11768
Dedicated to antique and vintage dolls and teddy bears, dollhouses, clothes, and accessories. Features: Articles by doll experts, "trips" to museums, information on doll shows and auctions, a calendar of events, and more.

Doll Artisan Magazine
www.dollmakingartisan.com
dollmaking@dollmakingartisan.com
N7450 Aanstad Road
PO Box 5000
Iola, WI 54945-5000
1-800-331-0038
Dedicated to authentic reproduction of antique porcelain dolls (1840–1920). Features: Question and answer section, tips, step-by-step projects, and technique detail.

Doll Costuming Magazine
www.dollmakingartisan.com
dollmaking@dollmakingartisan.com
N7450 Aanstad Road
PO Box 5000
Iola, WI 54945-5000
1-800-331-0038
Dedicated to the creation of authentic doll fashions. Features: Patterns, projects, instructions for making accessories, and a question and answer section.

Doll Magazine
www.dollmagazine.com
usoffice@ashdown.co.uk
32 Woodlake Drive SE
Rochester, MN 55904
507-288-5864
A full-color magazine for all doll collectors that includes the latest news, reviews, and many pictures.

Dollreader
www.dollreader.com
info@dollreader.com
Provides up-to-date information on antique, collectible, and modern dolls. Includes a question and answer section and columns by world-renowned doll authorities.

BOOKS

14th Blue Book of Dolls & Values
Jan Foulke, Howard Foulke (photographer)
September 1999, paperback, 336 pages
A price guide for antique and modern dolls organized in alphabetical order by manufacturer.

Antique Trader's Doll Makers & Marks
Dawn Herlocher
April 1999, paperback, 400 pages
A reference for authenticating prices and weeding out forgeries. Includes a description of each manufacturer's production history, doll mold characteristics, and illustrated examples of each maker's mark.

Care of Favorite Dolls: Antique Bisque Conservation
Mary G. Caruso
July 1999, paperback, 144 pages
Everything collectors need to know about the care of French and German bisque dolls. Includes step-by-step instructions on doll repair, eye repair, wig care, making cloth bodies, doll costuming, and accessories.

Collector's Encyclopedia of American Composition Dolls, 1900–1950: Identification and Values
Ursula R. Mertz, Otto J. Mertz (photographer)
November 1998, hardcover, 390 pages
Includes 850 color photographs, information on the technical aspects of production, history, tips on maintenance, and guidelines to determine quality and value of dolls.

Compo Dolls 1928–1955 Identification and Price Guide
Polly Judd and Pam Judd
May 2000, hardcover, 208 pages
A resource for identifying and pricing composition dolls. Contains never-before-published facts.

Designing the Doll: From Concept to Construction
Susanna Oroyan
March 1999, paperback, 160 pages
An in-depth guide to doll making that includes a variety of construction methods, tips on proportions, and much more.

Dolls and Accessories of the 1950s with Value Guide
Dian Zillner
September 1998, paperback, 168 pages
Includes over 590 color photographs of doll products of the 1950s including manufacturers such as Alexander, American Character, Artisan, Cosmopolitan, Effanbee, Horsman, Ideal, Mary Hoyer, Nancy Ann, Richwood, Terri Lee, Vogue, and more.

Dolls Aren't Just for Kids: The Ultimate Guide for Doll Lovers
Kathrine P. Peterson
January 2000, paperback, 209 pages
A book for doll lovers, artists, crafters, and collectors. Includes information on doll organizations, clubs, and events. Offers tips on photographing and promoting your dolls.

Doll Values: Antique to Modern
Patsy Moyer
April 2000, paperback, 352 pages
Includes doll manufacturer, doll history, marks, descriptions, and values.

The Handbook of Doll Repair and Restoration
Marty Westfield
September 1997, paperback, 288 pages
Step-by-step guide to doll repair and restoration without reducing value.

Madame Alexander: Collector's Dolls Price Guide, Volume 25
Linda Crowsey
April 2000, paperback, 96 pages
A reference for identifying and valuing Madame Alexander dolls.

GENERAL WEBSITES

Doll Collecting
www.collectdolls.about.com
Links to over 700 hundred doll related sites.

The Doll Net
www.thedollnet.com
Features online shops, bulletin boards, chat rooms, virtual cards, free patterns and tips, online classes, and much more.

Virtual DOLLS
www.virtualdolls.com
info@virtualdolls.com
117 South Cook Street #324
Barrington, IL 60010
Features contests, chat room, bulletin boards, and links. Get Doll eMagazine free.

CLUBS

The Doll Directory
www.thedolldirectory.com
A website of listings for doll clubs by state and manufacturer.

The National Antique Doll Dealers Association, Inc.
www.nadda.org
info@nadda.org
PO Box 5126
Lancaster, PA 17606
A non-profit organization dedicated to the advancement of education and ethics in doll collecting.

The National Institute of American Doll Artists
www.niada.org
niada@niada.org
An organization of doll artists and patrons dedicated to promoting the art of original handmade dolls.

The United Federation of Doll Clubs, Inc.
www.ufdc.org
ktwigg@ufdc.org
10920 North Ambassador Drive, #130
Kansas City, MO 64153
816-891-7040
The world's leading organization for everyone interested in dolls.

Doll Doctors

Antie Clare's Doll Hospital and Shop
www.antieclares.com
clare@antieclares.com
2543 Seppala Boulevard
North St. Paul, MN 55109
(651) 770-7522
Features: Antique to modern doll repair, frequently asked question section, before and after photographs, and dolls for sale.

The Art of Doll Restoration
www.sowatzka.com
7273 Kelly Drive
Lake Tomahawk, WI 54539
(715) 227-4591
Features: Doll restoration, gallery of restoration photographs, antique, reproduction and custom-made dolls for sale, doll restoration classes, doll repair, question and answer section, and appraisals.

A Doll's Dressmaker and Doll Hospital
www.dolllady14.tripod.com
dolllady14@cs.com
2435 North Schofield
Portland, OR 97217
(503) 735-9659
Features: Doll hospital, dolls, clothes and accessories, project or tip of the month, and doll parts and supplies.

Dolly Doc's Doll Shop and Hospital
www.dollydoc.com
thedollhouse@isol.com
315 Spruce Street
Mishicot, WI 54228
(920) 755-3080
Features: Dolls, bears and collectibles for sale, restoration, tips, and information. Join their club for free.

G&M Doll Restoration Seminars
www.gmdollseminar.com
Dwaine Gipe: dolldoc@suscom.net
JoAnn Mathias: dolldoc@pilot.infi.net
Features: Doll hospital, seminars, links, newsletters, and information about The Doll Doctor's Association.

Homestead Collectibles and Doll Hospital
www.homesteadcollectibles.com
dolldoctor@homesteadcollectibles.com
23483 Shepard Road
Clatskanie, OR 97016
1-888-763-5122
Features: Doll and toy restoration, frequently asked question section, doll stories, doll catalogs, accessories, and parts.

BIBLIOGRAPHY

Crowsey, Linda. *Madame Alexander Store Exclusives & Limited Editions: Identification & Values.* Paducay, Kentucky: Collector Books, 2000.

Foulke, Jan. *14th Blue Book: Dolls & Values.* Grantsville, Maryland: Hobby House Press, 1999.

_____. *Insider's Guide to Doll Buying & Selling: Antique to Modern.* Grantsville, Maryland: Hobby House Press, 1995.

_____. *Insider's Guide to German "Dolly" Collecting: Buying, Selling & Collecting Tips.* Grantsville, Maryland: Hobby House Press, 1995.

Herlocher, Dawn. *200 Years of Dolls: Identification and Price Guide.* Dubuque, Iowa: Antique Trader Books, 1996.

_____. *Doll Makers & Marks: A Guide to Identification.* Dubuque, Iowa: Antique Trader Books, 1999.

Judd, Pam and Polly. *Compo Dolls 1928–1955: Identification and Price Guide.* Grantsville, Maryland: Hobby House Press, 1991.

_____. *Handbook for Hard Plastic Dolls.* Grantsville, Maryland: Hobby House Press, 1999.

Karl, Michele. *Composition & Wood Dolls and Toys: A Collector's Reference Guide.* Norfolk, Virginia: Antique Trader Books, 1998.

King, Constance. *Collecting Dolls: Reference and Price Guide.* Suffolk, England: Antique Collector's Club Ltd., 1997.

Mandeville, A. Glenn. *The Golden Age of Collectible Dolls: 1946–1965.* Grantsville, Maryland: Hobby House Press, 1989.

McGonagle, Dorothy A. *A Celebration of American Dolls: From the Collections of the Strong Museum.* Grantsville, Maryland: Hobby House Press, 1997.

Mertz, Ursula R. *Collector's Encyclopedia of American Composition Dolls 1900–1950: Identification & Values.* Paducay, Kentucky: Collector Books, 1999.

Moyer, Patsy. *Doll Values: Antique to Modern.* Paducay, Kentucky: Collector Books, 2000.

Pearsall, Ronald. *A Connoisseur's Guide to Antique Dolls.* New York: Todtri, 1999.

Richter, Lydia and Joachim F. *Collecting Antique Dolls.* Cumberland, Maryland: Hobby House Press, 1991.